100 BEST IDEAS FOR Primary Language Arts

Written by
Carole MacKenthun, R.S.M.
and
Kathy Thoresen

Illustrated by Becky J. Radtke

Teaching & Learning Company

1204 Buchanan St., P.O. Box 10
Carthage, IL 62321

This book belongs to

_____

Dedicated to my Mother, Betty Leight — always in my heart.
Kathy

This book was developed for the Teaching & Learning Company by The Good Neighbor Press, Inc., Grand Junction, CO.

Cover illustration by Nancee McClure

Copyright © 1994, Teaching & Learning Company

ISBN No. 1-57310-001-3

Printing No. 987654321

Teaching & Learning Company
1204 Buchanan St., P.O. Box 10
Carthage, IL 62321

Table of Contents

The organization and structure of these ideas is based on a systematic literature program integrating reading, writing, speaking and listening with an emphasis on cultivating students' delight in language.

Dear Teacher,

The magical years of youth are rich in potential. A strong foundation for a lifetime of adventure is formed during early childhood. This "knowing-growing" period is developmentally prime. Young children exhibit notable behaviors of curiosity, activity, experimentation, imagination, imitation and enthusiasm. Meaningful early language experiences are vital for the development of the whole child.

This activity-based book offers teachers 100 of the best language arts ideas. Listening, speaking, reading and writing are the interrelated skills focused on in this book which help to provide a comprehensive language arts program that is fun and educational. Let us explore the essential parts more closely.

Listening

Hear Ye! Hear Ye! Did you know that students spend more class time listening than any other language skill? It is imperative that we as educators stress the importance of listening and let our students know we value it as an important learning tool. Listening activities such as show and tell, story time sharing and discussion should be incorporated into daily lessons to ensure proper auditory development. Encourage your students to become active listeners by being aware of voice tones, inflections, body/hand gestures and facial expressions. Listening activities guarantee that students will be better speakers, assisted in efforts of concentration and memory.

Speaking

As educators, we also must provide sufficient oral language opportunities. The proper development of these skills surely enhances the areas of reading and writing. Speech stimulation activities such as puppetry, creative centers, poetry recitation and singing allow students to organize thoughts and opinions, communicate clearly and listen attentively. Speaking activities can also foster self-esteem. Finger plays and storytelling can help students overcome shyness and fear of speaking in front of a group. Letting others know that what we have to say is important makes us feel special.

Reading

Reading in language consists of responding to questions based on a shared story, knowing word meanings, recognizing letters, predicting outcomes and sequencing. Reading activities such as sharing a book with a buddy, dramatizing stories, making self-created books and webbing techniques are some of the useful ideas found in this book to hone skills necessary for building a solid language arts program. Reading helps children become familiar with sentence structure and comprehension. It increases children's vocabulary and stimulates creative writing skills. Again, we see an interrelatedness with the other skill areas.

Writing

Writing can seem to be an arduous task for some children. Teachers can help their students become better writers by providing a "comfortable climate" and supplying ample writing time. Writing ideas can include book making, note writing, and drawing pictures. Journaling can act as a catalyst for children's writing and also can become a wonderful way to monitor a child's growth and self-expression. Sharing and displaying creative works promotes a positive self-image and a sense of accomplishment. These are needed ingredients for encouraging writers to "cook" and taste the pleasures of sweet success.

Development of Activity Pages

Each activity guides you step by step to the necessary completion of an idea. These steps include:

Skill and Subskill Divisions

At the top of each activity page will be listed that activity's area of focus and other skills being reinforced.

Materials

For each activity you will find a list of suggested materials that you will need to have on hand in order to complete the core activity as well as any extension activities.

Circle Time Talk

The suggestions contained in Circle Time Talk will serve as an introduction to your students and provide you with a clear understanding of the activity to follow.

Activity

Helpful, timely and language-enriched activities make this book shine. Sequential activity procedures guide the teacher and student to a successful language experience.

Extension Activities

This added resource gives various options to reinforce the core activity or take it one step further. Suggestions are given for self-guided learning experiences which can be adapted to meet the needs of your children.

Literature Links

Literature aids the development of listening, speaking, reading and writing abilities. Suggested books on each page are filled with rhythm, rhyme, repetition, humor and figurative language.

Fostering the love of language in the lives of children is fostering the development of the whole child. Daily incorporation of listening, speaking, reading and writing activities helps them internalize the importance of language in our everyday lives. Catch the spirit and dance of language! If you do, children will greet each day in your classroom with excitement and delight.

Sincerely,

Carole MacKenthun, R.S.M.

Kathy Thoresen

1. Teddy Bear Jump Rope Jingle

Materials
- jump ropes
- teddy bears
- graph paper
- teacher-made chart or big book
  of chant "Teddy Bear, Teddy Bear"

Circle Time Talk
Capture the interest of your students with this activity that will reinforce focused listening and speaking skills. Ask your students to bring their favorite teddy bear (or stuffed animal) to school. Read and discuss a selected story on bears while they cuddle their furry friends.

Activity
1. With your students, read through the preprinted chart for "Teddy Bear, Teddy Bear . . . "

   "Teddy bear, teddy bear, turn around.
   Teddy bear, teddy bear, touch the ground.
   Teddy bear, teddy bear, go upstairs.
   Teddy bear, teddy bear, drop your cares.
   Teddy bear, teddy bear, turn out the light.
   Teddy bear, teddy bear, say good night."

2. Talk through this rhythmic chant and repeat it until it is memorized.

3. Go outside or use your gymnasium to enjoy jumping rope.

4. If a student cannot jump rope, allow the "turners" to swing the rope side to side for the student to be able to jump over the rope instead of the rope going over his or her head.

Extension Activities
- Sing the following song to the tune "Mary Had a Little Lamb." Fill in the first two blanks with the name of a student and the next two blanks with adjectives to describe the teddy bear the student brought to school.

  _____ has a teddy bear, teddy bear, teddy bear.

  _____ has a teddy bear.

  It's _____ (brown) and _____ (furry) all over.

- Focused listening means helping children zero in on specific sounds or words that give direction. Jingles and singing games are a perfect way to reinforce this skill. You will also be providing a good learning opportunity for those students who love to put their whole bodies into learning.

Literature Links
Rappin' and Rhymin'. *Rosella R. Wallace, Ph.D. Arizona: Zephyr Press, 1992. (Cassette tape also available.) This book and tape contains raps, songs, cheers and smartrope jingles for active learning.*

Corduroy. *Don Freeman. New York: Puffin, 1976. A little girl buys Corduroy, a bear, with her piggy bank savings and has a friend for life.*

The Three Bears and 15 Other Stories. *Anne Rockwell. New York: Harper, 1984.*

Ira Sleeps Over. *Bernard Waber. New York: Houghton Mifflin, 1975. A boy sleeps over at a friend's house and decides if he should take along his favorite teddy bear.*

2. Talking Through Touch

Materials
- video camera and tape
- pictures of people communicating feelings through touch
- drawing paper
- large handprint shape

Circle Time Talk

Most times we tend to think that communication is either spoken, written or heard. We often forget the effect that "touch" has on communication. Discuss with the children the different meanings of "touch." For example, what does it mean when someone pats you on the back or shakes your hand? Choose volunteers to pretend to cry, be sick, sad or happy. Choose others to react to these emotions. Discuss how each child was comforted.

Activity

1. Videotape children spontaneously at a skill center or outside on the playground. Play the tape for the students so they can watch themselves acting and communicating with others. Share how their "touches" helped them communicate.

2. Younger children can draw a picture on drawing paper or inside the shape of a handprint to show how they shared their feelings through touch. Write their statement at the bottom.

3. Older students can role-play the different kinds of "touch" gestures and let classmates guess what they are trying to communicate.

Extension Activities

- This may be a good time to discuss the differences between "good" touches and "bad" touches. Perhaps you can invite a doctor, nurse, police officer or family counselor to school to aid in your discussion. Encourage children to bring this idea home to the family for further discussion.

- Touches can make us feel silly, relaxed, anxious, etc. Prepare bowls of Jell-O™, cold spaghetti, shaving cream, flour, sandpaper, brushes, etc. Blindfold students and let them "touch" items in the prepared bowls. Capture their facial expressions with a camera. Place pictures in a classroom scrapbook. This is a fun way to remember these enjoyable "touching moments."

- Buy "Hug Coupons" to give to students. Order from: Once upon a Planet, 39 Norwood Road, Port Washington, NY 11050, or make your own.

Literature Links

The Blind Man and the Elephant. *Lillian Quigley. New York: Charles Scribner's Sons, 1959. This old Indian fable relates how six blind men seek to understand an elephant through the gift of touching. Each man must learn to listen to one another, realizing that each has an important part of the entire picture.*

Pat the Bunny. *Dorothy Kunhardt. New York: Golden Books, 1962. An ideal book geared to involve a child's senses.*

Hugs. *Alice McLerran. New York: Scholastic, 1993. This book contains "hug" stories of precious children that are written in a rhyming text that will delight all who read it.*

3. Act Naturally

Materials
- yarn
- index cards
- construction paper (optional for masks)
- animal masks (optional)

Circle Time Talk
Creative dramatics is a wonderful and different way to interest children in books. Dramatics comes naturally to children because their play is already full of pretending. Explain to the children that they are about to meet various animals such as geese, goats, horses, cows and bears. Have volunteers show how these animals "talk" and "act." Compare how these animals behave in the story *and* in real life.

Activity

1. Choose either a story from the Literature Links section or any story that contains a lot of animals (and animal action).

2. Pass out masks or premade necklaces (made from yarn and index cards) with the names of the books' animal characters on them.

3. Read the story again. This time your students will act out what you read.

4. Choose new students to act out the story without the book being read. Remember, creative dramatics is a nonrehearsed activity. Let the children act naturally!

Extension Activities
- The following actions are done by some of the animals in the suggested stories: walk, skip, hop, gallop, trot and run. If possible, go outside and ask different volunteers to demonstrate each of the actions. Then allow all the students to participate. When you are finished, give yourself a big bear hug!

- Visit a farm or zoo. Ask children to notice how the animals "act" and "talk." Upon returning, have the children draw a picture of a favorite animal they saw during the field trip. Write a sentence to describe the drawing. For example, "Today I saw a duck waddle and quack." Bind students' work with yarn or brass fasteners to make a class book. Give the class book a title such as *Animal Antics* or *A Day at the* _____.

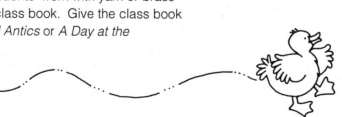

Literature Links
Ask Mr. Bear. *Marjorie Flack. New York: Macmillian Pub. Co., Inc., 1932. This modern classic tells of a boy searching for the perfect birthday present for his mother. His animals friends help him end his search.*

Polar Bear, Polar Bear, What Do You Hear? *Bill Martin, Jr. New York: Henry Holt and Company, 1991. Eric Carle beautifully illustrates this book about zoo animals that make distinctive sounds children can imitate.*

4. "Knot" a Story (What a Yarn!)

Materials
- ball of thick, brightly colored yarn

Circle Time Talk
Read one of the Literature Links storybooks to your circle (or any other fun and lively fairy or folktale). Explain to the students that many times when stories begin with "Once upon a time," they are fairy tales or fables. Encourage the class to volunteer to mime their favorite fairy tale characters and allow their classmates to guess who they are.

Activity
1. Prepare for this activity by taking strands of yarn and attaching them to each other forming large knots. Roll the yarn in a ball.

2. Seat the students on the floor in a circle and hold the ball of yarn. Tell them that you are going to begin a "Once upon a Time" story and unroll the yarn as you go along. When you come to a knot, you will pass the yarn to the next student, who will in turn continue the story.

3. For example, you might begin by saying, "Once upon a time, a little girl named Tiffany rode her bicycle over the rainbow . . ."

4. If your students get stuck and can't think of an imaginative way to continue the "yarn," have them pass the yarn back to you and proceed with a suitably outrageous story segment. This will get the ball rolling again!

Extension Activities
- Have prereaders share a different ending to a famous fairy tale and illustrate it using colored chalk or tempera paints.

- Inspire your readers to write an original fairy tale in which two different famous characters meet in the same scene.

Literature Links
The True Story of the Three Little Pigs. *John Scriezka. New York: Viking Press, 1989. This delightful tale relates the wolf's version of his experience with the three little "porkies." Peels of laughter will be heard as each page is read and the clever artwork is enjoyed.*

The Ugly Duckling.
Hans Christian Andersen. New York: Charles Scribner's Sons, 1964. This favorite story teaches an important lesson in self-image. It shares an insightful lesson that some of us need more time to grow and bring out the beauty that is within.

5. No "Phonies" Allowed

Materials
- real or toy telephone
- note paper
- pencils

Circle Time Talk

Using a real or toy telephone as a prop, carry on a mock conversation about something fun, exciting or different that happened in your school or classroom recently. Make it brief. Then ask your students "Do you ever use the telephone? Who do you call on the phone? How do you answer the phone when someone calls? What do you say when your parents are away or unable to come to the phone?" Stress with the students how to respond courteously and with clear diction. Do the students know their own phone numbers? Impress upon them the importance of knowing this information in case of an emergency.

Activity

1. Using a telephone, pretend you are talking to someone in the class. Compliment this student about a great assignment that was completed or a talent he or she shared with the class.

2. Encourage students to volunteer to call someone in the class and praise the student for a job well done or good behavior.

3. Have younger students practice using the telephone to learn the proper way to answer and respond to calls.

Extension Activities

- Almost everyone has occasionally dialed a wrong number. Tell about a funny experience you had doing this, and ask students to relate similar circumstances.

- Think about other phone numbers students might like to dial. For instance, numbers of sports stars, singers, book characters, etc. Have students use the phone to express what they might like to say to these people.

- Choose characters from a book such as the ones in Literature Links and have students dramatize them talking to each other on the telephone.

Literature Links
Frog and Toad Are Friends. *Arnold Lobel. New York: Harper Junior Books, 1970. Two best friends share humorous adventures as they quarrel, make up and plan activities together.*

Blueberries for Sal. *Robert McCloskey. New York: Viking, 1948. A little girl and bear cub wander away from their mothers who are picking blueberries. Each mistakes the other's mother for its own.*

6. Riddle Me This!

Materials
- riddle or joke book(s)
- hat or ball

Circle Time Talk
Everyone likes a good laugh once in a while! This activity encourages the shyest of children to speak out and have fun. Ask the children if they know what a joke or riddle is; then allow children to give examples. Show them your sense of humor by reciting your own joke. You wouldn't be teaching if you didn't have a great sense of humor–right?

Activity
1. Before you begin this activity, be sure all the children have a joke or riddle to share. If not, photocopy a page from one of the Literature Links suggestions for them to memorize. Do the activity when everyone has something to share.

2. Have children sit in a circle passing a hat (on head) or ball (in hand) chanting this nonsense line "Ta Ra Ra Boom De Ay." Repeat this line seven or eight times, each time saying it a little faster.

3. When the chant is finished, whoever is wearing the hat or holding the ball gets to tell his favorite joke, rhyme or riddle.

Extension Activities
- Present a comedy hour program "Jokes R Us" for the parents or school. Encourage children to memorize skits, jokes, limericks, riddles, etc. Everyone will enjoy the show!

- Take your show on the road! Visit a children's hospital or a retirement home to cheer up those who are hurt, sick or lonely. Laughter is the best medicine!

Literature Links
Committing jokes or riddles to memory comes naturally to children. Children will show how clever and witty they are, building self-confidence and a sense of humor. The books below contain a wealth of humor for your students to read and memorize.

Bennet Cerf's Book of Animal Riddles. *Bennet Cerf. New York: Random House, 1959.*

Unidentified Flying Riddles. *Joanne E. Bernstein and Paul Cohen. Niles, IL: A. Whitman, 1983.*

Knock Knocks: The Most Ever. *William Cole. New York: Franklin Watts, Inc., 1976.*

7. Colors of My World

Materials
- strips of colored paper (brown, black, white, green, blue, red, yellow, purple and pink)
- pictures of eyes, ears, nose, mouth and hands
- tape recorder
- chalkboard, chalk

Circle Time Talk
Here's another great activity that will reinforce focused listening and involve the whole child. Gather your group around you and pass out strips of colored paper. Ask them to listen to the song "Parade of Colors" by Hap Palmer (*Can a Cherry Pie Wave Goodbye?* Freeport, New York: Educational Activities, 1991). Explain that when they hear their color mentioned in the song, they need to stand up. Play the song again and allow children to switch their color strips with their neighbors. After the song, ask students what things in their world are the same color as the strip they are holding.

Activity
1. Explain to children that they know about color by using their senses. Show a picture (or draw on board) of eyes. Ask children, "How does blue look?" Replies may include water, sky, jeans and blueberries. List words on board under picture of eyes.

2. Follow the same pattern for the rest of the senses.
   Examples:
   How does blue sound? *(swooshy, like waves)*
   How does blue smell? *(yummy like blueberry pie, sweet like Kool-Aid™)*
   How does blue taste? *(cool like ice)*
   How does blue feel? *(wet like water, soft like blueberries)*

3. Substitute for blue any other color you wish to reinforce using the senses.

Extension Activities
- Older students will have fun writing similies for color. For example, "Her eyes are as blue as a pool." Then have them illustrate their similies!

- Younger students will have fun mixing colors to make green, purple, orange, etc. Use white icing and food coloring for this activity, spread the results on graham crackers and eat up! Yum!

Literature Links
Best Story Book Ever. *Richard Scarry. New York: Western Publishing Company, Inc., 1968. This book is a wonderful collection of poems, stories and rhymes containing themes of animals, alphabets, colors and others of special interest to children.*

Brown Bear, Brown Bear, What Do You See? *Bill Martin, Jr. New York: Holt, 1983. This rhyming story poses the question, "What Do You See?" The answer leads to additional questions pertaining to colors and animals.*

8. Feelings

Materials
- pictures of facial expressions showing a wide range of emotions
- drawing paper (folded in fourths; in each box write:
  "I feel _____ when _____.")
- crayons and pencils

Circle Time Talk

Talking and writing about feelings is an empowering thing for all children. It gives them the tools they need to grow beyond using their fists in anger or being mute with despair. During circle time, read a book that deals with a wide range of emotions, from happy to sad. Discuss the book with your students, asking if they have ever felt the way the character(s) in the book felt or if they would feel differently in a similar situation.

Activity

1. Share pictures you have prepared. Discuss the ways people show their feelings and the way the people look.

2. Write all the "feeling" words your students suggest on a piece of graph paper labeled "FEELINGS." Allow students to demonstrate how people look when they are angry, happy, etc.

3. Read the story *The Giving Tree* or another story dealing with feelings.

4. After the story is read, ask the students to identify the feelings of the characters in the story. Add new "feeling" words to the chart or circle the words if they are already on the chart.

5. Hand out prepared drawing paper. Your students can complete the sentence in each box with a "feeling" word discussed in the story. They can then draw a picture to match each sentence. Have your students share and display their work.

Extension Activities

- **Inside-Out Kids.** Have your students lie down on butcher paper and trace around them with a wide marker. If your students can write, have them fill the inside of their figure with images and words that describe their feelings. Prewriters can fill their figures with hand-rendered images and pictures cut from magazines.

- Reinforce listening and reading comprehension skills by asking questions about how characters from favorite storybooks felt during certain parts of the story. Example: How did Max feel when his mom sent him to his room without his supper?

Literature Links
Quarreling Book.
Charlotte Zolotow. New York: Harper & Row, 1963. Quarreling in a family on a rainy day makes everyone suffer. All ends well when the father returns home happy.

The Tenth Good Thing About Barney.
Judy Viorst. New York: Atheneum Publishers, 1972. Dealing with the death of a pet is not easy. This book can help children cope with feelings of grief as they hear a little boy discover ten good things to say about his cat at the funeral.

The Giving Tree.
Shel Silverstein. New York: HarperCollins, 1974. As time passes, a boy and a "giving" tree form a lasting friendship.

Feelings. *Aliki. New York: Greenwillow Books, 1984. This is a good book that suggests ways of dealing with feelings.*

9. Let's Do Drama Creative Center

Materials

- costumes
- puppets
- pencils, paper (drama center)
- chalkboard, chalk (drama center)
- typewriter
- masks
- phone
- erasers or cloth

Circle Time Talk

Explain to children that this is an activity they will do on their own. Discuss what drama and role playing are. Ask a student to pretend to be the teacher, and you pretend to be a student (what a *classy* move!). Stress the importance of putting things back where they belong. **Note:** Dramatic play occurs naturally when the drama center is near the art center.

Activity

The following is a list of roles and activities the children can pretend to be and do to help reinforce writing skills.

Waitress/Waiter—take orders, write menu
Nurse/Doctor—write prescriptions, keep patients' records
Game Show Host—keep score
Mom/Dad—write phone messages, phone numbers, grocery lists
Teacher—write assignments/lessons on board, keep record book
911 Operator—record emergencies, names and addresses
Secretary—take messages, write/type letters
Veterinarian—keep records of pets, height, weight
Author—write a book
Mechanic—list things wrong with automobile

Extension Activities

- Invite a "career person" in to share how important writing clear messages is to his or her job. Discuss what would happen if someone took a wrong message or wrote an unclear note.

- See a local production. Afterward, discuss the characters and how they "played their roles." Recall props and scenery used to enhance the play production. Maybe you can put on a play of your own. Also discuss the differences between acting at the drama center and acting in a play.

Literature Links
Amelia Bedelia.
Peggy Parish. New York: Scholastic, 1970. Amelia is a lovable maid who is a walking disaster. She shares a humorous story about being a maid.

My Mother the Mail Carrier. *Inez Maury. New York: Feminist Press, 1976. Lupita is a child from a one-parent family. She discusses this and her mother's job as a mail carrier.*

Miss Nelson Is Missing. *Harry Allard. New York: Scholastic, 1978. Poor Miss Nelson has trouble controlling her class. Suddenly a substitute teacher takes her place, and she changes the class's behavior.*

10. Reader's Theatre

Materials

- boot box
- shelf paper or construction paper
- X-acto knife (for adult use only)
- fax paper roll

- ¼" (.6 cm) dowels
- tape, glue, crayons
- scissors

Circle Time Talk

This activity provides children practice in speaking in front of a group. It also helps them sequence and organize thoughts into a story. Talk with children about possible topics for a story. Examples might be My Day at School, Our/My Family Vacation, My (6th) Birthday or The Happiest/Worst Day of My Life. Show the children that they are going to make a "theatre" using pictures to tell a personal story.

Activity

1. Ask parent helpers to come in to assist you with this project.

2. Separate children into groups. One group will draw pictures on the fax paper related to personal experiences that can be retold in a story format. Another group will decorate the outside of the boot box with shelf or construction paper. (Parents can assist by cutting paper to fit boxes, cutting slots in the boxes where the paper will be fed through and cutting the dowels.)

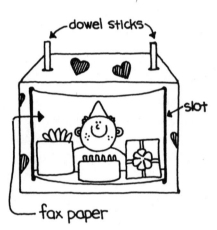

3. Have children thread the fax paper through the slots in the box and tape the beginning of the roll to the empty dowel.

4. Roll the pictures onto the empty dowel while each child stands to tell his or her story as each frame is shown. There is room for many stories on one roll of fax paper, so store your tiny theatre in one of your centers so that this can be an ongoing activity for your students.

Extension Activities

- Change the story in your theatre to draw: new illustrations for a favorite story (i.e. *Goldilocks and the Three Bears*), a cartoon adventure for your favorite character or illustrate a well-liked song or poem.

- Create an alphabet theatre. Write uppercase and lowercase letters, then illustrate. Sing or read your alphabet story.

11. Free to Be Something Else

Materials

- box of patterns of recognizable shapes such as a dog, cat, sun, moon, tree, shoe, pencil, star
- construction paper
- pencils
- scissors, glue
- yarn, buttons, cotton balls, glitter or sparkles

Circle Time Talk

Ask students if they ever wondered how it would feel to be a bird flying gracefully over the ocean or a star twinkling in the night sky. Encourage them to pretend to be something other than themselves. Have them share responses.

Activity

1. Have students choose a favorite pattern from the box; trace it onto construction paper and cut it out.

2. Tell children to pretend to be their objects and talk about themselves. For example: "I am furry and as white as a cloud. The sun warms me, and I purr. With my paws I walk ever so silently so no one knows where I am." *(cat)* Have students write their thoughts in the shape of their chosen object. You will need to write on the pattern for prewriters. Details can be added with crayons, and items such as yarn and buttons can be glued on.

Extension Activity

- Have students make a simple paper bag puppet of their character. This puppet can then talk about his or her typical day. This activity can be a big help to shy children who dislike reading aloud for the class.

Literature Links

Nonhuman objects take on human characteristics and describe their feelings in the following poems.

"I'd Like to Be a Lighthouse" by Rachel Field and *"The Table and the Chair"* by Edward Lear from **Dilly Dilly Piccalilli.** *Edited by Myra Cohn Livingston. New York: Margaret McElderry Books, 1989.*

Any Me I Want to Be. *Karla Kuskin. New York: Harper & Row, 1972.*

"Square as a House" in **Dogs and Dragons, Trees and Dreams.** *Karla Kuskin. New York: Harper & Row, 1980.*

12. Searching for Sounds

Materials
- tape recorder and tape
- drawing paper
- crayons
- magnets
- chalkboard
- chalk
- chart paper and marker

Circle Time Talk
This activity will help children recognize and describe sounds in their environment. Demonstrate sounds for the children to guess. For example, bark like a dog, ding-dong like a doorbell or ring like a telephone. Discuss how sounds help send messages. For instance, a crying baby could mean he or she is hungry, tired, frightened or hurt.

Activity
1. Explain to the students that they are going to pretend to be detectives searching for sounds. In order to be dynamite detectives, they need to block out all other distractions and concentrate on listening for sounds.

2. Before becoming detectives, talk about what kinds of sounds you might hear on your journey. Give children drawing paper for them to draw the sounds. Children might draw teachers or students talking, a book dropping, pencils sharpening, birds chirping, leaves rustling, etc.

3. Take a "detective walk" inside or outside of the school. (Be sure to tell the students where you will be searching for sounds before they draw their pictures.) Tape-record sounds on your walk. Remind the children that detectives are very quiet while they are searching for clues (in this case, sounds).

4. Put the drawings on chalkboard with magnets. Play the tape from the search. Identify all recorded sounds. As each sound is identified, place a check mark next to each picture drawn that has the same sound heard on the tape.

5. Discover the sounds on the tape that were not drawn and vice versa.

6. List all the sounds heard on the search (according to the tape) on chart paper labeled "Our Search for Sounds."

Extension Activities
- Make a large graph of the predicted sounds using the students' drawings and compare. Example: How many students thought they would hear a teacher compared to how many students thought they would hear footsteps? Evaluate items which had most, least, etc. Label graph "School Sound" or "Nature's Calling," etc.

- Encourage children to make their own sound tape at home. Allow the students to bring in their tapes for the class to identify the "sounds at home."

Literature Links
The Mystery of the Giant Footprints.
Fernando Krahn. New York: Dutton, 1977. Children will enjoy playing detective to discover and solve the mystery of giant footprints in this wordless picture book.

The Very Busy Spider. *Eric Carle. New York: Putnam, 1984. The sounds of the barnyard animals does not disrupt the spider from spinning her web. Students will enjoy listening to the specific sounds the animals make.*

Sound All Around.
Fay Robinson. Chicago: Children's Press, 1994. In this book the author discusses the nature of sound, items that make sound, how sound travels and pitch. Beautiful photographs illustrate this informative book!

13. Pail O' Pictures

Materials
- pail
- pictures of a potato chip, a chair, ketchup, salt, toothpaste, a juice box, a sneaker, a pencil, a stapler, a jelly bean, a tire, a cup, a birthday candle, a telephone, a train, a computer, a snack cake, etc.
- drawing paper, construction paper
- crayons

Circle Time Talk
Teach the students the song "Pick a Bale O' Cotton" *(The Corner Grocery Store* by Raffi Troubadour Records, 1979) using the words:

Jump down, turn around
Pick a pail of pictures.
Jump down, turn around
Pick one today.
O Lordee, pick a pail of pictures.
O Lordee, pick one today.
O, <u>Molly</u>, pick a pail of pictures.
O, <u>Molly</u>, pick one today.
<u>Molly</u> and <u>Scott</u> gonna pick a pail of pictures.
<u>Molly</u> and <u>Scott</u> gonna pick one today.

Activity
Gather the needed pictures, glue each one onto construction paper and put them in a pail. Ask for a volunteer to pick one while the class sings the song. The teacher will substitute student names for the underlined names. The student will then talk without stopping on the chosen topic for ten seconds. (Time can be added as proficiency increases.) The speaker can describe it, discuss what it's made of, if she likes it, if she's ever used it, etc. Another volunteer can be called, and this student's name is added to the song also.

Extension Activities
- Take a small box and put two objects in the box. Have students create a "crazy" conversation about these items. This would be ideal for partners. Think – Pair – Share!

- Create a video strip using one or more of the objects. Provide drawing paper and crayons to make a wordless picture story.

Literature Links
These are ideal books for use with inanimate objects.

Any Me I Want to Be. *Karla Kuskin. New York: Harper & Row, 1972.*

The Pancake. *Anita Lobel. New York: William Morrow, 1978.*

Freight Train. *Donald Crews. New York: Greenwillow, 1978.*

14. Uninvited Birthday Guests

Materials
- party favor bag
- slips of paper with different occupations written on them (doctor, secretary, teacher, nurse, artist, musician, author, illustrator, mail carrier, fire fighter, police officer, salesperson, food server, etc.)
- drawing paper
- crayons

Circle Time Talk
Have the students discuss what they do at a party. What games do they play? What do they eat? What time of the year do they attend them?

Activity
Fill the party favor bag with names or pictures of people who would not normally be invited to a children's birthday party. Have a student choose a name and act like the person he chose. Another student will choose the name "Host" and try to guess the occupation of the uninvited guest. For example: The uninvited guest can ask the host how he or she feels (doctor) or if he or she would like more to eat (food server). The "Host" rotates so all students get a chance to guess the characters. Simple snacks can be provided!

Extension Activities
- Design a welcome mat for the uninvited guests to make them feel "welcome." For example, a musician would have musical notes drawn on the rectangular sheet of drawing paper with the word *WELCOME!*

- Make a "wanted" poster for uninvited guests. Include a picture (from a magazine) or a sketch of the person.

Literature Links
Striped Ice Cream.
Joan Lexau. New York: Lippincott, 1968. Becky wants striped ice cream for her birthday party and gets a lovely surprise as she turns eight years old.

Birthday Parties Around the World.
Barbara Rinkoff. New York: Barrows, 1967. Recipes, games, favors, decorations and birthday customs of 23 countries are described.

OCCUPATION _____

WANTED FOR _____

LOOKS LIKE _____

LAST SEEN _____

REWARD _____

15. So Silly!

Materials

- tempera paint
- paintbrushes
- art paper
- pencils

Circle Time Talk

Read a book with at least one silly character. Children have very creative imaginations. This activity will let their imaginations run wild. Ask the children what a silly character or creature would look like. Let them explain their answers. Ask them to act how their character or creature would behave at a birthday party or if they didn't get their own way.

Activity

1. Challenge the students to paint silly characters or creatures. As they work, they should think of a name and personality type for their creations.

2. After the painting is complete, have the children write its name and description on the paper. Younger children can dictate this information while you write it on their papers.

3. Stimulate creative thinking in older children by listing questions on the chalkboard for children to write about. If your students are prereaders, these questions will be topics for discussion. Questions may include:

   - Where does it live?
   - What types of food does it like?
   - How did it get here?
   - What does it do?

4. Display the pictures and writings for all to see. Or you may wish to bind pictures and writings into a class book labeled "Such Silly Characters." Display the book on a table.

Extension Activities

- Take a walk with your creation. Go on an adventure and tell about it.

- Give children free time to play with their creations. Imagine "Zork" meeting the "Mud Monster." Watch out for real creative play.

- There are so many silly things to talk about with your students! Encourage them to think about what makes something "silly." Does it make them laugh? Talk about jokes, riddles and the things they see on television that make them laugh.

Literature Links
C Is for Curious: An ABC of Feelings.
Woodleigh Hubbard. San Francisco: Chronicle Books, 1990. Twenty-six adjectives help demonstrate the actions of zany animals. Children can share if their "silly" characters act that way, too!

On Beyond Zebra.
Theodore S. Geisel. New York: Random House, Inc., 1955. An alphabet book for those who don't want to stop at Z.

16. Puppet Play Creative Center

Materials
- drawing paper
- glue, stapler
- craft sticks or tongue depressors
- Styrofoam™ balls, corks or sponges
- thumbtacks or pins with large heads (for puppet eyes)
- stage (file folders make great instant stages)

- crayons, markers
- scissors
- yarn
- socks, handkerchiefs or gloves
- buttons
- paper bags
- potatoes, yams, carrots, turnips

Circle Time Talk
Puppets provide a fine outlet for more effective speech and creative expression. Children who are shy or practice English as a second language will find it easy to speak through the puppets. Practice finger plays such as "Fine Speckled Frogs" or "Where Is Thumbkin?" to prepare finger movement in puppets.

Activity
1. Students will enjoy dramatizing Mother Goose poems and fairy tales with puppets. Older students might enjoy writing their own plays or stories and have their buddies help make puppets needed for characters.

2. Here are some suggestions on how to make puppets.

Stick:
- Staple simple drawings to tongue depressors.
- Drape an 8" or 9" (20.32 or 22.86 cm) cloth square over a stick, insert into a Styrofoam™ ball. Add pins for eyes and cloth or paper for nose and mouth and yarn for hair.
- Pin original drawings to a large cork and insert a stick into the base for movement.
- Insert sticks into vegetables to create a variety of characters.

Hand:
- Slip hand into a sock, work fingers to create a mouth, fit toe of sock with cardboard and glue and decorate as necessary.
- Make a hole large enough for the child's finger in a Styrofoam™ ball. Decorate the ball. Drape cloth over hand and insert index finger in hole.
- Draw or glue a face at the bottom of a paper bag, making sure the mouth is under the crease. Open and close crease to show how the puppet talks.

Extension Activities
- Once your students have mastered the use of puppets, put on shows for parents, other classes and other special events.

- Make a puppet book. First make a paper bag puppet of a story character or famous person. Attach 3" x 5" (7.62 x 12.7 cm) writing paper to the puppet with a stapler. Students can write a summary of the story or write facts about a famous person's life and have the puppets tell the story.

Literature Links
Easy to Make Puppets. *Frieda Gates. Chippewa Falls, Wisconsin. Harvey House, 1976. This book focuses on making puppets for students ages K-3.*

Finger Rhymes.
Marc Brown. New York: E.P. Dutton, 1980. Practice finger plays with students using this age-appropriate finger rhyme book.

17. Speak and Spin

Materials
- paper fasteners
- paper clips
- plastic container tops
- paper plates
- markers

Circle Time Talk
Read the students a selection from the Literature Links or review a previously read story. Ask them to rate the story and give reasons for their answers.

Activity

1. Create your own spinner games by taking four plastic tops and covering them with small paper plates measured to fit them. Divide the circles into quarters and use permanent markers to write various categories on them. Make a hole in the center of each and attach a paper clip to the spinner circle by running a paper fastener through the paper clip.

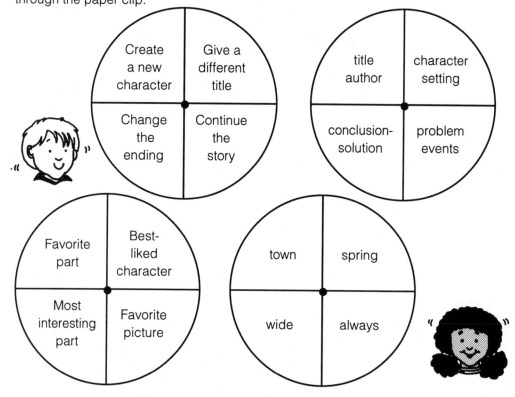

Create a new character | Give a different title
Change the ending | Continue the story

title author | character setting
conclusion-solution | problem events

Favorite part | Best-liked character
Most interesting part | Favorite picture

town | spring
wide | always

2. Divide your class into groups. One child from each group will spin the paper clip and must answer the question asked. After five minutes, rotate the groups.

Extension Activities
- Have students use the spelling words in a sentence; identify vowels, consonants or syllables; create rhyming words.

- Story starters can be completed by students. For example, in one quarter write: I came to school one day and a clown was sitting in the teacher's chair.

Literature Links
Why Mosquitoes Buzz in People's Ears: A Wise African Tale. *Verna Aardema. New York: Dial Books, 1975. This rhyming folktale tells about the adventures of a mischievous mosquito.*

Umbrella. *Taro Yashima. New York: Viking Press, 1958. Moma, a Japanese girl, awaits the rain to use her new umbrella and red rubber boots.*

18. Poetry Puppets

Materials
- paint sticks
- cottage cheese container lid (for use as a circle pattern)
- 1 circle of paper for each student
- crayons or markers
- Scotch™ tape

Circle Time Talk
Young children love poetry. They take enthusiastic pleasure in the musical rhythm, the richness of alliteration and onomatopoeia, and the zest for language that a good poem communicates. Prior to circle time, choose two to three poems with several animals or characters (so your students will have more to choose from when they make their puppets). Gather your circle around you, and read the poems you have chosen.

Activity
1. Invite each student to choose a character from the poems you have just shared. In order to have as many different puppets as possible, you may want to ask, "Who would like to be the unicorn? Who would like to be the eagle?," etc.

2. The children can illustrate their characters with markers or crayons on the circles of paper you prepared earlier.

3. Tape the circles to the paint sticks using two criss-crossed pieces of tape.

4. Read each poem again, and when the students hear the name of their character read, they can hold their puppet up and repeat the name of their character.

Extension Activities
- Give a smaller group of students two puppets each. Reread the poem you have created your poetry puppets for. Help students learn right and left by prompting them at the appropriate time to hold up the character in their right hand or their left hand.

- Invite your students to dramatize the poem in their own words using their poetry puppets. The ability to retell a story is an important reading skill.

Literature Links
The Sky Is Full of Song. *Lee Bennett Hopkins. New York: Harper Junior Books, 1983. Many outstanding poets are recognized in this book of 38 short poems that help visualize the scenes of each season. Spin a poem and enjoy!*

Where the Sidewalk Ends. *Shel Silverstein. New York: Harper & Row, 1974. A poetry book students can't put down and always choose to read over and over.*

"Keep a Poem in Your Pocket" from ***Something Special.*** *Beatrice Schenk de Regniers. New York: Harcourt, 1986. A delightful poem to share with a friend or recite alone to fill your mind with dancing thoughts.*

19. Wishes upon Stars

Materials

- selections from Literature Links or books and videos in which the characters make wishes
- yellow construction paper stars – 9" to 10" (22.86 to 25.4 cm) with lines to write on
- banner that says "Wishes upon Stars"
- markers

Circle Time Talk

"Star light, star bright, first star I see tonight . . . I wish I may, I wish I might, have this wish I wish tonight." Most of us remember this sweet poem from our childhood. Try this simple activity with your students and encourage all kinds of good, language-related skills: brainstorming, creative thinking, discussing and sharing thoughts. When you first gather your circle around you, share the "Star Light" poem with your group. Invite them to learn the poem, too, so you can say it together as a group. Then read one or two of the suggested storybooks to your circle. When you have finished reading, talk about how the wishes affected the characters and the outcome of the story. Invite your students to talk about *their* wishes. This would be a good time for you to share one or two of your own wishes with your group.

Activity

1. Encourage each child to think of something he would like to wish for.

2. Invite them to write their wishes on stars. You will need to do the writing for your prewriters.

3. If time permits, each student can also draw a picture of what it would be like if her wish was fulfilled.

4. Attach each star to the top of the picture and display all of your wishes on a wall or bulletin board under the banner "Wishes upon Stars."

Extension Activity

- Brainstorm with the students what kind of wish they would wish for the following: Mom, Dad, a friend, a teacher, the school, homework, the Earth . . . .

Literature Links
Sylvester and the Magic Pebble.
William Steig. New York: Simon & Schuster, 1969. Sylvester the donkey is granted many wishes once he finds a magic pebble that must be held in his hand.

William's Doll.
Charlotte Zolotow. New York: Harper, 1985. William wishes he had a doll to play with instead of the ordinary "boy toys," such as a basketball or trains. His grandmother succeeds in making his wish come true and teaches an important lesson to all.

"A Wish" from **The Way I Feel Sometimes.** *Beatrice Schenk de Regniers. New York: Houghton Mifflin Co., 1988.*

Three Wishes. *Paul Galdone. New York: McGraw Hill, 1961. An old tale is told of a woodsman, his wife and three wishes.*

20. Shape Up!

Materials
- drawing paper
- crayons
- samples of shapes being reinforced

Circle Time Talk
Using words to describe shapes and sizes is a prewriting skill that you will be able to nurture using this activity. However, some simple ideas will need to be discussed with your group prior to this activity. Read one of the Literature Links selections (or any other book that is rich with shapes and bright colors) to your students, reviewing circles, squares, triangles and rectangles. Be certain that they understand the directions *up, down, middle, top, bottom, left* and *right*. To introduce movement to this activity, create shapes like triangles, squares and rectangles with your students by arranging a few students at a time on the floor.

Activity
1. Children should look around the room to find something shaped like a square, circle, triangle, etc. Distribute drawing paper with the name of a shape written at the bottom. Have each student in the class draw a certain number of that shape on that paper.

2. Prepare several teacher-made direction cards giving directions to the placement and color of various shapes. For example, "Draw a small, red circle inside a large, yellow square." Pair the students and sit them back to back on the floor or on chairs. One student will give the other directions where to place a particular shape on the back of his or her paper. For example, "Put a red circle in the middle of the paper." Then students reverse roles. After each student has a chance to listen and draw, pictures should be compared with their partners'. Have a group discussion on how you can communicate better with a partner.

Extension Activities
- Prepare a teacher-made "direction tape" giving similar directions using various shapes, colors and numbers. For example, the teacher would ask the listener to draw a large, blue circle in the center of the paper. Then draw a medium-sized, red square inside the blue circle. Finally draw a small, green triangle in the center of the square.

- You can reinforce number, letter or color recognition using the same activity.

- Have students draw a picture of an animal or a vehicle, using one particular shape. The book *Cut and Create! At the Zoo* (© 1994 by Teaching & Learning Company) is a great resource for this kind of activity.

Literature Links

Arrow to the Sun: A Pueblo Indian Tale.
Gerald McDermott. New York: Viking Press, 1974. Have the children pick out the various geometric shapes in this beautifully illustrated and entertaining book.

Watch Out! A Giant!
Eric Carle. Cleveland and New York: The Williams Collins + World Publishing Company. This illustrator/author has a style that includes simple shapes and bright, clear colors. This book has die cuts in the shapes of circles and squares to enable you to reinforce these shapes to your students.

Shapes and Things.
Tana Hoban. New York: Macmillan Co., Inc., 1970. The author/artist uses white on black and creates the impression that white shapes are alive. Extensive examples are given!

Shapes, Circles, Triangles and Squares.* Tana Hoban. *New York: Macmillan, 1974. Tana uses black and white photographs of everyday objects to help children generalize about shapes they see.*

21. The Storyteller's Chair

Materials
- enjoyable stories to share
- comfortable storyteller's chair

Circle Time Talk

Encourage students to talk about their favorite stories. When did they first hear it? Who told the story? What part of the story did they like the best? Take students over to the storyteller's chair. Explain to them that whoever sits there will get to share a story with the class. Everyone will listen carefully to the speaker.

Activity

1. Before the circle time activity, decorate the storyteller's chair by adding a soft cushion, streamers, ribbons or pictures from previously read stories.

2. Prepare to share a favorite story with the students by reading it three or four times to yourself until you have internalized the basic story line and practiced it. As you tell the story aloud, make it enjoyable to hear by using an expressive voice.

Extension Activities

- Prereaders can be chosen to sit in the storyteller's chair and share a favorite story with the class. Choose a few students each day until all have had a chance to be the storyteller.

- Have students dramatize a favorite fairy tale such as "Jack and the Beanstalk" or "The Three Little Pigs," etc.

- Students can also use the storyteller's chair to read a favorite story or poem to the class.

- One of the wordless picture books listed in Literature Links would be ideal for students to create their own text using the pictures to stimulate them.

Literature Links
The Snowman.
Raymond Briggs. New York: Random House, 1978. This book would surely inspire winter thoughts about a favorite playtime friend.

Deep in the Forest.
Brinton Turkle. New York: Dutton, 1976. This wordless picture book is a reverse of "Goldilocks and the Three Bears." Children will enjoy creating the text as seen through the eyes of a little bear cub.

22. Box a Story

Materials
- large box
- props
- costumes
- hats
- scenery

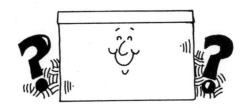

Circle Time Talk

Make stories come alive by "box"ing them up. Inside a decorated box have props, hats, costumes and scenery pertaining to a particular story. These items can be collected and made by parents. Just ask! Talk to the children about how scenery and props can make storybooks more interesting and enjoyable to listen to and watch.

Activity

1. Choose a story that is a favorite among your students or choose one from the Literature Links section.

2. Children can wear costumes, hold props and scenery while listening to the story. Each time the story is read, allow children to wear or hold something different.

3. If you have a shortage of costumes or props, then throughout the story say a "magic" word, phrase or nonsense sound to indicate that these materials should now be given to someone not wearing or holding any story-related material. Children won't mind sharing in this story.

4. After the students have listened to the story, they can dramatize the story using the items in the prop box. Decide who will play each character. You may need to change "actors" several times throughout the story so each child gets a chance to participate.

Extension Activities

- Place odd items, props, hats, etc., in the "story box." Allow children to create their own stories or imitate storybook characters off the cuff!

- Brainstorm with children, if they had a "magic" box of their own, what would they put inside it to keep it safe and why? Children can write their personal thoughts in their journals.

Literature Links

"Box" these favorite children's stories and make them come alive again and again!

Caps for Sale. *Esphyr Slobodkina. New York: Harper Junior Books, 1947.*

Frederick. *Leo Lionni. New York: Pantheon, 1966.*

Where the Wild Things Are. *Maurice Sendak. New York: Harper Junior Books, 1963.*

23. Hello, Jell-O™!

Materials

- boxes of flavored gelatin (amount depends upon class size)
- mixing bowls and spoons
- boiling water and cold water
- oiled cake pan and waxed paper
- chart paper
- cookie cutters

Circle Time Talk

Ask students if they have ever assisted their parents in cooking or baking. What did they make? How did a recipe aid them in preparing the food? What is their favorite recipe? Pretend to be gelatin sitting in the refrigerator, being carried to the table and being eaten!

Activity

1. Gather students around a large table with the necessary items needed to make gelatin. Have the recipe written on chart paper to share with the class.

2. Read the directions and ask for volunteers to assist you in preparing the gelatin. For example: Mix 4 regular boxes of flavored gelatin in a bowl. Add 2½ cups (600 ml) of boiling water. Stir the mixture together. Pour the mixture into an oiled cake pan. When it is cool, use cookie cutters to cut gelatin into shapes.

3. Give each student a gelatin shape. Discuss how it feels. What words might describe it? Write these answers on chart paper. Students might use such words as *slippery, shaky, wiggly*, etc.

4. Finally, eat it and enjoy!

Extension Activity

- Prepare an edible alphabet with the class. Mix together equal amounts of peanut butter, honey and powdered milk. This mixture makes a dough you can eat. Distribute portions on waxed paper and have each student create a letter she has have been assigned. Students can then walk around the room and observe each other's creations. Have them sit in a circle and eat the alphabet together!

Literature Links

Stone Soup. *Marcia Brown. New York: Charles Scribner, 1947. Hungry soldiers trick the village people into getting a meal. All share ingredients to make a delicious soup.*

The Popcorn Book.

Tomie de Paola. New York: Holiday House, 1978. Recipes and facts about popcorn blended with information and humor.

24. Show and Tell Twist

Materials
- index cards, chart paper
- envelopes
- pencils, crayons
- relevant sharing item for "show and tell"

Circle Time Talk

This activity works especially well if you are teaching in thematic units. Encourage the children to bring in an article to share that relates to your theme. For example: If your theme centers around rabbits, the children can bring in carrots, real or stuffed bunnies, pictures or photographs of rabbits. Older students can go to the library and research rabbit facts. You can even dance the Bunny Hop! What a "hare"-raising idea! Surprise students with your own show and tell. The children can always use a good model for sharing time.

Show and Tell Song *(to the tune of "I'm a Little Teapot.")*

1. Let's have show and tell now,
   You and me.
   Who has a sharing,
   For us to see?

2. Let's have show and tell now,
   You and me.
   We'll go in order,
   From A to Z.

Activity

1. Review the specific theme or subject you are currently studying. Keep a running list of facts about that particular subject. A discussion about fact and opinion can be easily integrated.

2. Encourage children to share their articles. If children are slow to share, ask thought-provoking questions to promote their speech.

3. After the sharing, give each student an index card. Encourage them to write a special note to whoever shared (or listened nicely) saying something positive about their sharing (or behavior). Nonwriters may share their comments orally and take an index card home for parents to help write the special note.

Literature Links
What Mary Jo Shared. *Janice Udry. New York: Whitman, 1966. Mary Jo brings in a unique show and tell for her classmates—her father!*

Let's Go to the Post Office. *Naomi Bucheimer. New York: Putnam, 1957. This book shows children what to expect to see on a trip to the post office.*

The Jolly Postman. *Janet and Allan Ahlberg. New York: Little Brown, 1986. The postman delivers real letters from famous characters such as Goldilocks and Cinderella. Excellent source to introduce certain writing skills.*

4. Decorate a bulletin board to look like a mailbox labeled "Mail Center" or "Communication Center." Place decorated envelopes (ask your local card store for donations) on the board so children can "mail" their special notes.

This board can be kept up all year for different uses. Children can "mail" party invitations and papers that need special attention. Teachers can "mail" notes to parents or awards to children.

Remind students to check their "mailboxes" daily. Monitor the students' boxes to make sure that everyone receives mail.

Extension Activities

- Visit a post office. See what happens to letters after they're put into the mailbox. Send a thank-you letter to the post office. When writing the letter, encourage students to recall the events of their trip from beginning to end. This will reinforce letter writing and sequence skills.

- Have children design a new and original stamp. Ask the art teacher, principal, etc., to judge and award a prize to the most original stamp. Children will enjoy finding out what philatelists do! They collect stamps, of course!

25. The Listening Post

Materials
- pole decorated with streamers (Your hardware store will cut a 2½" [6.35 cm] PVC pipe to length for you.)

Circle Time Talk
Show the students the "listening post," and tell them whenever you hold it they should put on their "listening ears." Have them mime putting on a large pair of ears. Encourage them to listen carefully to any sounds around the room, such as another teacher talking nearby, a bird chirping, etc.

Activity
1. Each day when it is time to line up for lunch, recess or dismissal, hold the listening pole. Choose one of the following game-like starters and remind the students that everyone will have a chance to be "leader of the line." Say to them, "Line up if . . ."
   - your age is an even number
   - you have a winter birthday
   - you play a musical instrument
   - you did an act of kindness today
   - you have curly hair
   - you have a fruit in your lunch box
   - you have brown eyes
   - you're wearing green
   - you have a pet

2. Try some of these also: "Line up if you can tell me . . ."
   - a "bl" blend
   - a compound word
   - a circle shape in the room
   - the sum of 2 + 2
   - the name of a noun in the classroom
   - the name of the president of the United States
   - five even numbers starting with 2
   - how many months in a year
   - the days of the week
   - the primary colors

Literature Links
The House That Jack Built: A Picture Book in Two Languages. *Antonio Frasconi. New York: Harcourt, 1958. This is a picture book in which cumulative links are seen throughout the words which help Jack build his house in order.*

Look What I Can Do.
Jose Aruego. New York: Scribner, 1971. In this book two animals compete to see who is the best leader.

Extension Activities
- Now have students try lining up with a partner who matches one of the descriptions below. Say, "Find a classmate who . . ."
  - has the same first letter in your name
  - has a missing tooth
  - has the same color eyes as you
  - wore a jacket to school
  - answered a question in class today
  - rides a bus to school
  - has the same color hair as you
  - doesn't have a partner

- Use the "listening post" when making special announcements or greeting a student on a birthday or an important achievement in class.

26. Cloudy Thoughts

Materials
- flannel board
- pieces of white felt
- scissors
- sidewalk chalk

Circle Time Talk

What images in nature are as mutable as clouds? They provide the perfect vehicle for this exercise in fantasy and tapping inner voices. The perfect setting for this Circle Time would be outside, on a partly cloudy day. With your group, observe the clouds around you, and encourage your students to use their imaginations to create images. Read one of the suggested titles from the Literature Links section or any other book that has pictures of clouds that are strongly suggestive of other things. *It Looked Like Spilt Milk* is perfect for this activity.

Activity

1. Preread the book *It Looked Like Spilt Milk.* If this title is unavailable to you, you may choose any book with a variety of images, and this activity will still work well.

2. Trace images from the book onto white felt.

3. Distribute the white felt objects to various students. Allow each student to identify his or her shape.

4. Next read the book to the students and invite each one to place the felt shape on the flannel board when the students recognize the object in the story.

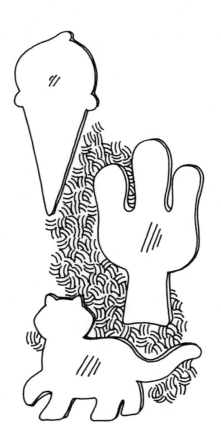

Extension Activities

- Go outside and discover how clouds can make different shapes in the sky. Have students identify them and draw shapes on the pavement using sidewalk chalk.

- Demonstrate how differently we each see the same thing: Draw an odd-shaped cloud on the chalkboard. Ask your students what this cloud reminds them of. Write down as many responses as your students offer.

Literature Links

Cloudy with a Chance of Meatballs. *Judi Barrett. New York: Macmillan Book Company, 1978. In this riotously funny book, amazing things fall from the clouds! Your students will love it!*

"Clouds" from **Sing a Song of Popcorn.** *Christina Rossetti. New York: Scholastic, Inc., 1988. Here's a lovely poem that speaks to the magic in children and grown-ups' hearts.*

It Looked Like Spilt Milk. *Charles G. Shaw. New York: Harper & Row, 1947. Clouds take on various shapes and remind the author of ordinary objects, such as a birthday cake, an ice-cream cone, etc.*

27. Flannel Board Box Creative Center

Materials
- flannel board box–To make: connect 4 pieces of plywood (approximately 18" to 24" [45.72 to 60.96 cm] square) with hinges; then cover with flannel. Attach Ziploc™ bags to the back with staple gun.
- various flannel shapes such as circles, hearts, bunnies, squares, etc.
- tape recorder and tape
- Ziploc™ bags
- teacher-made answer key to activity

Circle Time Talk
Explain to the children how important listening skills are to their learning. Cite examples of everyday activities that involve careful listening. Play an echo game with children. Example: clap, snap, clap, snap. Children will imitate your example. Each time, make the echo a little more challenging. Show children flannel board box, recorder and tape. Explain how they will be used. Remind them of responsibility and cooperation.

Activity
1. Prepare a tape recorded sequencing activity for the center. Allow four students to work at the same time. An example of a sequencing activity might be:

    "Number one—first place one circle on the board. Next, place two squares next to the circle. Last, place one circle next to the squares." Repeat the pattern out loud. "Check the answer key; then go on to number two. Press *stop* now."

2. Begin with simple patterns, then work toward patterns that become more complicated. All the flannel board pieces, answer keys and tapes should be placed in the attached bags for easy storage.

Extension Activities
- Children can use this center to continue practicing sequencing without the tape recorder. Prepare sequencing cards for children to copy to reinforce one-to-one correspondence skills.

- Encourage parents or upper-grade students to record the children's favorite stories. Prepare flannel board pieces (characters and setting) that go along with the story. Store tape and story parts in the attached Ziploc™ bags. Change stories every so often.

- Prepare flannel board songs, too! Try "Old MacDonald," "I Know an Old Lady" or "The Alphabet Song."

Literature Links
These favorites make wonderful flannel board stories.

Chicken Little.
Steven Kellogg. New York: William Morrow, 1985.

The Little Red Hen.
Paul Galdone. New York: Clarion, 1973.

The Mitten. *Jan Brett. New York: G.P. Putnam, 1989.*

28. Inside Self, Outside Self

Materials
- boxes
- magazines and catalogs
- crayons, paint, markers, glue
- index cards

Circle Time Talk

Discuss with students objects that appear one way on the outside and another way on the inside. A gift, for example, has wrapping paper on the outside and contains something hidden inside. An oyster shell looks completely different from the pearl that lives within. Have students describe one another by outward appearances only. Then have them share something about themselves that others cannot see. For example, one student might love his grandmother very much or become embarrassed when reading in class.

Activity

1. Distribute boxes to students along with magazines and catalogs, and have them draw visible things about themselves on the outside of their boxes. These things might include hair color, eye color, glasses or braces that they wear; the kind of home they live in; what kind of pet they have; members of their family and hobbies they have.

2. On the inside they will fill their boxes with pictures, words and sentences of personal qualities that might not be visible to others. For example, a picture of pizza could symbolize their favorite food. A nighttime picture could represent their fear of darkness.

Extension Activities

- Invite the children to wear their clothes inside out one day while sharing something of their "inside self."

- Write a poem using the pattern

  My outside self . . . (likes lots of friends)
  My inside self . . . (likes to be alone reading a book)

  Repeat the pattern with as many qualities as possible.

Literature Links

Outside-Inside Poems. *Arnold Adolf. New York: Lothrop, 1981. These poems accompanied by black and white drawings, depict thoughts and feelings about being young and growing.*

Let's Go Swimming with Mr. Sillypants.

M.K. Brown. New York: Crown, 1986. In this story, Mr. Sillypants overcomes his fear of swimming lessons.

29. Chalk Talk Creative Center

Materials
- chalkboard easel
- white and colored chalk
- sidewalk chalk
- erasers or cloths
- paintbrushes
- sponges of various shapes
- magnet stories

Circle Time Talk
The chalkboard center is a haven for students to work independently on their affective development. Remind students of the rules when using this area. Explain the materials and how to use them creatively, not haphazardly.

Activities
The following is a list of ideas the children can complete while using the chalkboard easel.

1. Practice writing letters using water and a paintbrush.
2. Trace shape sponges or dip sponges in water and pat them on the board to make a design.
3. Make a rainy day design. Draw squiggly, curvy lines on the board. Wherever there is an empty space, draw a design with different colored chalk.
4. Tell a story with a friend using magnet characters. (Glue a magnet to the back of each character.) Draw your own scenery.
5. Practice listening and communication skills by letting two children stand on either side of the easel. A third child gives directions as to how, where and what to draw. Each child draws that object. Then compare drawings. Example: "Draw a large circle in the middle of the page. Draw a triangle inside the circle, touching the sides."
6. Draw a new ending to a story or illustrate a song or nursery rhyme.
7. Make a file box with different drawing activities. Example:

- Once there was a table. *(Draw a circle.)*
- The table had four triangular legs. *(Add 4 triangles.)*
- There was a bowl on the table. *(Add a circle.)*
- There were two beans in the bowl. *(Draw 2 dots in circle.)*
- There were two beans on the table, too.
  (Draw 2 dots above circle.)
- Suddenly a hungry pig crept into the picture and ate them. (Oink!) *(Add a squiggly tail.)*

8. Practice your spelling words.
9. Make crazy characters out of numbers.
10. Draw a self-portrait.

Extension Activity
- Advertise what your students are reading. On a chalkboard easel, write the title of the book, the author and a sentence to describe the beginning and another sentence to describe the middle. Write a sentence like "What do you think is going to happen?" Illustrate and place the easel in the library or lunch room. This might encourage students to take out this book to find out how the story ends.

Literature Links
Here's a list of titles that will provide fun and simple activities for your Chalk Talk Creative Center:

Ed Emberly's Big Purple Drawing Book. *Edward Emberly. Boston: Little, Brown and Company, 1981.*

Ed Emberly's Drawing Book of Faces. *Edward Emberly. Boston: Little, Brown and Company, 1975.*

Ed Emberly's Big Green Drawing Book. *Edward Emberly. Boston: Little, Brown and Company, 1979.*

30. Wacky Words

Materials
- books or poems using sound words (onomatopoeia)
- comic books or cartoon pages

Circle Time Talk
Drop a paper clip or coin on the floor. Ask students to think of a word that resembles this sound. Tell them that some words in our language are formed from a natural imitation of sounds. Examples: Kerplop! Smash! Clunk! Inform your group that this is called "onomatopoeia." Repeat the word as a group several times just for fun!

Activity
1. Distribute copies of a cartoon or comic book page in which a few sound words are included.

2. Your prereaders can listen as you read the selection aloud. Repeat it again and have them stand up when they hear a "wacky" word.

3. Beginning readers could assist you by creating the sound of the wacky word as it is being read.

Extension Activities
- Students can invent their own words by using the everyday noises of a school bus, a vacuum cleaner, the wind, a pencil being sharpened, etc. Illustrate them by drawing the chosen object and the sound in a word bubble.

- Play a variation of the game Duck, Duck, Goose. Have students sit in a circle. One student is "It" and taps the heads of those in the circle, saying a sound word. (Example: Clunk!) Then "It" substitutes the word *goose* instead of the sound word, "Goose" tries to catch "It" before "It" takes "Goose's" place in the circle. "Goose" then is "It." If "It" is caught, he or she sits in the center of the circle until another student takes his or her place.

Literature Links
The following books are filled with onomatopoeia.

"Weather" and "A Matter of Taste" from **Jamboree: Rhymes for All Times.** *Eve Merriam. New York: Dell, 1984.*

More Sound Words. *Joan Hanson. New York: Lerner, 1979.*

Crash! Bang! Boom! *Peter Spier. New York: Doubleday, 1972.*

31. Snacking Sequence

Materials

- 1 package instant chocolate pudding
- 1 8-ounce (226.8 g) tub of whipped topping
- 1 package chocolate sandwich cookies
- 2 cups (480 ml) cold milk
- gummy worms and frogs
- paper or plastic cups
- plastic bag
- large bowl
- wire whisk
- chart paper
- rolling pin
- sentence strips
- crayons
- writing paper
- pencils

Circle Time Talk

Ask students to describe their favorite snacks. What steps do they take to prepare them? When do they eat them? What are the necessary ingredients?

Activity

1. For a special day, plan a "dirt dessert" to share with students. Gather the necessary ingredients and have students stand around a large desk or table for this activity. Explain to the students that this is how we make dirt dessert:

   First we crush the cookies in a zipper plastic bag with a rolling pin.
   Next we pour milk into a large bowl. Add the pudding mix and beat with a wire whisk for 2 minutes. Let stand for 5 minutes.
   Then we stir in the whipped topping and add ½ of the crushed cookies.
   Finally we fill the cups with pudding mixture, top with remaining crushed cookies, add gummy worms and/or frogs and refrigerate for 1 hour.

2. While pudding is in refrigerator, distribute writing paper, pencils and crayons to students and direct them in writing their own steps for making a favorite snack. Use the form on the right which can be written on the chalkboard or overhead projector. Encourage students to add illustrations, staple together and create their own *Class Snack Book*.

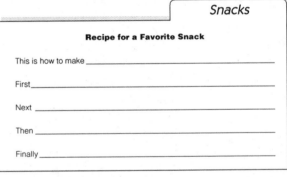

Snacks

Recipe for a Favorite Snack

This is how to make _____

First_____

Next _____

Then _____

Finally_____

Enlarge and duplicate

Extension Activities

- Use this same form to write other sequential strips for everyday activities, such as making a bed, doing homework, setting the table, playing a game, feeding your pet, etc.

- Distribute sentence strips to students. Have them write each step of an activity on a separate strip. Choose one student's completed activity strips. Four volunteers then go to the front of the room, each holding one strip from the sequence. Classmates can assist them in putting the sentence strips in sequential order.

- Create a "step book." Take three sheets of paper and overlap them, leaving a 1" (2.54 cm) margin at the bottom of each page. Hold the pages so they remain overlapped and fold. The book now has six pages. Staple through all layers of the book next to the fold at the top. Write the title on the outside page. Write on each step and illustrate under each flap.

Literature Links
The Cookie Book.
Eva Moore. New York: Scholastic, 1973. Fun to make, easy to bake cookie suggestions and recipes for every month of the year.

Book Cooks. *Janet Bruno. CA: Creative Teacher Press, 1993 (K-3 edition). This book features classroom cooking activities inspired by favorite children's books.*

32. Egg Treasure Hunt

Materials
- plastic eggs (1 for each child)
- holiday stickers
- variety of candy
- index cards
- marker

Circle Time Talk
This activity encourages children to follow directions in sequence and have fun while doing it. Imagine that! Before beginning activity, enjoy a game of Simon Says or Mother, May I to practice oral listening skills. Then explain that they are going on an Egg Treasure Hunt, but in order to find the treasure they need to follow directions very carefully.

Activity
1. Before beginning this activity, have prepared plastic eggs filled with goodies and sealed with stickers. Write each child's name on an egg and hide them.

2. On each child's desk place an index card with step-by-step directions for how to find their treasures.

3. The child takes the card and a pencil, reads the first direction and checks it off when completed. If one child is going alone, then no pencil is needed, just watch his or her steps as he or she reads the card. You may want to dictate directions to younger students.

4. When all steps are completed correctly, the child should have found his or her treasure. Be sure that the treasure is in plain sight by the last step.

5. Remind children that if they find a treasure that is not theirs, to leave it alone for the right owner to claim.

6. At last, enjoy the treasure.

Extension Activities
- Older students' directions may include words like *north, south, east* and *west.* Younger students' directions may include words like *under, over, left* and *right.*

- Children may want to refill and redecorate the egg for a student in another class. Provide index cards for them to write step-by-step directions. Happy hunting!

Literature Links
The Tale of Peter Rabbit. *Beatrix Potter. New York: Warne, 1903. Peter Rabbit does not follow his mother's directions and goes in Mr. MacGregor's garden. Children learn the importance of following directions.*

Nate the Great and the Phony Clue.
Marjorie Weinman Sharmat. New York: Coward-McCann, 1977. Children learn the value of following clues step-by-step. Nate's detective work is interfered with by two boys and a phony clue.

33. Tell-Me Gram

Materials
- note paper to look like telegrams
- pencils
- chart paper

Circle Time Talk

Ask students if they ever received a telegram. Explain to them that a telegram is a short message delivered quickly. The sender has to pay for each letter of the telegram, so brief is better! Encourage students to think of a short message they would like to send to their parents, grandparents, a distant friend, a sick classmate, etc. Share responses with each other.

Activity

1. On large chart paper, reproduce a telegram-like form. Explain that the students will try to summarize a story today and write it like a short message. For example, in the story *The Elves and the Shoemaker*, the message could be:

   Elves find clothes!

2. Distribute paper to students and ask them to write a telegram that summarizes the main idea in one of their favorite books. After the class has completed this activity, students could volunteer to read their telegrams and others could try to guess the title of the book.

Extension Activities

- Students could create telegrams for other lessons: defining spelling words; summarizing homework assignments; giving main idea of today's lesson.

- Students can write short messages to sick classmates about the work they missed. These notes can be put in student mailboxes (see Mail Center on page 25).

- Encourage students to send a "tell-me" gram to a family member before leaving for school. Messages can be left in lunch bags, briefcases, coffee cups or suit pockets.

Literature Links

The following books are good selections for detecting the main idea.

Seven Blind Mice.
Ed Young. New York: Philomel, 1992. Seven blind mice cooperate in finding a solution to their problem.

Fables. *Arnold Lobel. New York: Harper, 1980. Well-known fables relate short, powerful lessons to young and old.*

34. A Character's Tea

Materials

- juice, cups
- cookies, napkins
- costumes (provided by students)
- outline of a character map
- pencils

Circle Time Talk

Making literature come alive in your classroom is a gift given to your students that they will never forget. Talk with your students about their favorite storybook characters. Find out why that character is their favorite, how is that character different from or the same as them. Discuss also if that character has been in more than one book. Did that character act the same in all stories? What were the titles of those stories, and who are the authors?

Activity

1. Children will choose their favorite character to study. Topics to study could be the feelings they share, physical appearance, actions they perform, places they go and objects they use.

2. Assist children in making a character map. This map will "flesh out" the items mentioned above. Some children may choose the same character and may work together.

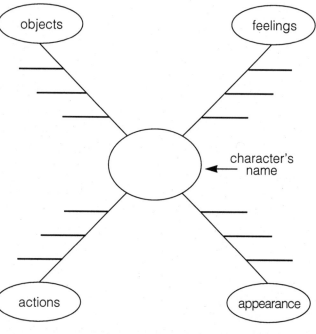

3. After completing the character study, the children will dress up as that character. Other children will guess what characters their classmates are and also try to guess from which books the characters came.

4. Invite the characters to tea. Students will talk with one another in character. Imagine Curious George meeting Miss Nelson!

Extension Activity

- Visit other classrooms and let the other students guess each character. Maybe they will meet one for the first time!

Literature Links

The following books contain "character" titles. They make character study fun and interesting.

Madeline. *Ludwig Bemmelmans. New York: Penguin, 1977.*

Petunia. *Roger Duvoisin. New York: Knopf, 1950.*

Little Red Riding Hood. *Jakob Grimm and Wilhelm Grimm. Retold by Trina S. Hyman. New York: Holiday House, 1983.*

Old Mother Hubbard and Her Dog. *Paul Galdone. New York: McGraw, 1960.*

35. Silver Penny Thoughts

Materials
- pennies covered with aluminum foil
- art paper and crayons

Circle Time Talk
Ask students to think of some favorite places they've visited. Encourage them to describe what they saw, why they enjoyed the experience and what memories are stored in their minds.

Activity
1. Distribute a "silver" penny to each student. Tell them that with this penny they can enter Fantasyland! Recite this verse as you give them their coins:

> Here are your silver pennies.
> Hold them tightly in your hands.
> You must have these silver pennies
> To enter Fantasyland!

2. Lead the students in a visualization to prepare them for imagining a trip to Fantasyland. Distribute art paper, crayons and pencils beforehand.

Step 1: Dim the classroom lights. Play an instrumental tape such as *Silver Wings* or *Fairy Ring* by Mike Rowland (Music Design, Inc., 207 E. Buffalo, Milwaukee, WI 53202). Say the following sentences slowly and pause after each phrase (. . .).

> Today we are going to take a journey in our minds . . . In order to prepare for our journey, you must put your feet flat on the floor . . . Close your eyes . . . Take a minute to relax and clear your mind of other thoughts . . . Now we are going to take some slow, deep breaths . . . Gradually fill your chest with all the air you can . . . Hold it . . . Slowly exhale and let out all the old air . . . Now breathe this way again . . . All the way in . . . All the way out . . . Deep breath in . . . Deep breath out . . . Now just pay attention to your normal breathing . . . Don't forget to keep your eyes closed as I continue . . . .

Step 2: Visualization

Now we are going to take a special journey . . . Don't forget to hold onto your silver penny as we start . . . It is a bright, sunny day . . . Feel the warmth of the sun . . . Hear the chirping of the birds in the sky . . . Listen to the babbling of a clear brook . . . Look at the lovely yellow daisies in the meadow . . . Lean over to smell them . . . Continue to walk along until you come to a brightly colored rainbow near the end of the path . . . Use your silver penny to catch a cloud with a silver lining . . . Just relax and feel this white, fluffy cloud as it lifts you somewhere over the rainbow . . . Dangle your feet while sitting on it and relax . . . The cloud floats you to your exciting fantasyland . . . It begins to descend slowly and waits until you have jumped off . . . Take a moment now to use your senses of sight, touch, hearing and smell to get to know this magical place . . . (Give students about a minute or two, depending on their maturity.) Now it is time for us to leave . . . Hold onto your silver penny and wish yourself back to the classroom . . . At the count of five, open your eyes . . . 1, 2, 3, 4, 5!

Step 3: Follow-Up

Have students take the paper and crayons already on their desks and draw their favorite scene from their journeys.

Step 4: Sharing

Encourage students to share their favorite scenes from their adventures with the class.

36. "Heart"y Baskets

Materials
- construction paper
- materials for decorations
- crayons
- glue
- paper
- scissors

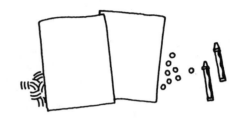

Circle Time Talk

The purpose for this activity is to encourage focused listening, an important tool for learning. Give volunteers oral directions for them to follow. Example: "Stand up, turn around three times, then sit down and cross your legs. Discuss the importance of listening to and following directions. Also, discuss the consequences of not listening to and following directions.

Activity

1. Give each child two 6" x 8" (15.24 x 20.32 cm) pieces of construction paper and one 1" x 10" (2.54 x 25.4 cm) piece of construction paper. (This will make a small basket.)

2. Instruct the students to:

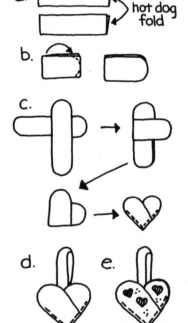

   a. Fold the two smaller pieces of construction paper in half, widthwise (like a hot dog as opposed to a hamburger fold).

   b. Hold the ends together and round off the corners.

   c. Lay the two pieces open on the desk, one on top of the other, cross and fold back together. This will form a heart shape. Staple together.

   d. Staple on a handle.

   e. Decorate the basket using crayons, tissue paper, glitter, etc.

Extension Activities

- Make pink, red and white baskets around Valentine's Day for easy distribution of valentine cards. For younger students who have difficulty reading names, assign numbers to children. Numbers should be placed on cards and baskets.

- Cut out pictures from magazines or catalogs that begin with the letter *B*. Place pictures in baskets and share.

Literature Links
Origami: A Children's Book.
Irmgard Kneissler. Emeryville, CA. Children's Press, 1992. This is a fun book instructing students how to make other paper folding activities.

Sadako and the Thousand Paper
Cranes. *Eleanor Coerr. New York: Putnam, 1977. Sadako, a young Japanese girl, sick in the hospital, tried to fold one thousand paper cranes, hoping the gods would grant her wish to be well again. She folded 644 cranes before she died, and her classmates folded the rest in her honor.*

37. Sayings That Drive Me Up a Wall!

Materials
- chalkboard
- drawing paper
- chalk
- crayons

Circle Time Talk

Ask students if they have ever heard the expression: He drives me crazy! What do they think it means? Explain that sometimes words that we speak mean something other than what the phrase actually says. This is called an idiom.

Activity

1. List these expressions on the board:

- I'm sitting "on top of the world."
- He is in "hot water."
- You're the "apple of my eye."
- It's "a piece of cake."
- The child was "all ears" when the teacher shared the story.
- This lesson was "over my head."
- The student has a "big head" after winning the contest.
- My brother was "all thumbs"!
- Mom was "up to her ears" in work.
- You're "driving me up a wall."
- She's a "chicken" when it comes to flying.
- We all need a "pat on the back" once in awhile.
- My grandmother was "tickled pink" with her birthday present.

2. Discuss the meanings with the students and have them choose one to illustrate. Distribute art paper and direct them to write the idiom and draw the humorous (literal) meaning on the front side; on the back they are to write the true meaning of the expression. Students then share their work with their classmates.

Extension Activities

- Students can mime idiomatic expressions and have classmates guess what they are.

- Create a bulletin board entitled "Busy Body Idioms" and include on it expressions such as:

  - She "talked her head off" last night at the party.
  - His "heart wasn't in it," but he tried his best.
  - My friend told me something crazy, and I think he's "pulling my leg."
  - Dad paid "an arm and a leg" for my new bike.
  - Our neighbor "gave me the cold shoulder."
  - We have been "on our toes" lately.
  - The coach "stuck his neck out" for us again after the game.

Try to use students' names in sentences you write. They will enjoy seeing their names in print.

Literature Links

Humorous idioms and illustrations are a delight to all readers. These books are excellent sources of idioms in print.

The King Who Rained. *Fred Gwynne. New York: Windmill Books, 1970.*

Chocolate Mousse for Dinner. *Fred Gwynne. New York: Windmill Books, 1976.*

Amelia Bedelia. *Peggy Parish. New York: Scholastic, 1970.*

38. Can-a-Sound

Materials
- 8 empty coffee cans with lids
- small objects: lima beans, marbles, paper clips, sand, bells, etc.
- self-adhesive paper

Circle Time Talk
This activity will allow students to identify similar sounds. Ask your students what sounds they would hear during a particular season at the park, beach, zoo or the seashore. Ask the students if any of these sounds are similar.

Activity
1. Cover coffee cans and lids with self-adhesive paper.

2. Place objects in coffee cans. Use all eight cans. Be sure that half the cans have the same items in them as the other half. For example, you might put marbles in two cans, beans in two cans, paper clips in two cans and sand in two cans. Put a self-correcting mark on the bottoms of the matching cans.

3. Line up the cans on a table. Choose a volunteer to guess which two cans make the same sound. If the cans chosen do not make the same sound, another student may take a turn. If they do make the same sound, have students try to guess what is inside. Do this until all cans have been matched.

Extension Activities
- Encourage children to make up onomatopoeic words for the sounds they heard in the cans. Discover if there are things in our environment that make the same sounds.

- Play an echo game. Ask a student to make a city or country sound. Ask another student to make an echo of the original sound.

Literature Links
Choose one of these stories and have the students determine what sounds could be heard in their various settings.

The Little House.
Virginia L. Burton. New York: Houghton, 1948. Setting: city and country.

One Small Blue Bead. *Byrd Baylor Schweitzer. New York: Macmillan, 1965. Setting: desert.*

Milton the Early Riser. *Robert Kraus. New York: Messner, 1981. Setting: jungle.*

White Snow, Bright Snow. *Alvin Tresselt. New York: Lothrop, 1947. Setting: winter.*

39. Poetry Party

Materials

- pictures of food
- 1 or 2 big bags of crunchy potato chips
- cooperation of some classroom parents

Circle Time Talk

Here's your chance to share your love of language and the rhythm of poetry with your students. Introduce this activity by reading two or three poems about food. Talk about food; the way it tastes, looks, feels, smells. Open a bag of crunchy potato chips, and let your group discuss the way it feels to enjoy a potato chip. If this is your time to lead some movement activities, read one of the food poems and let your students hop, jump, sway and clap to the rhythm of the poetry.

Activity

1. Read several poems about food to your students.

2. Do some webbing about food. This allows emerging and prewriters to map out their thoughts on the subject in an organized, understandable manner.

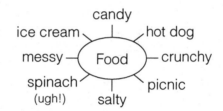

3. Introduce the idea of a poetry party. In order to keep this from mushrooming into something unmanageable, you'll need to suggest easily prepared foods for the party from the poems you have just read.

4. Ask some room parents to provide the foods needed for your poetry party. It can be as simple as peanut butter, jelly and bread.

5. After the students have completed their food, do some more webbing about the poetry party.

Extension Activities

- Using the food webs created earlier, create some of your own food rhymes with your students. If your students are prereaders, chant or sing the rhymes. Go out on the playground and jump rope to your rhymes.

- Readers and writers can write poems about their favorite foods and illustrate them. Hang these in the classroom for all to see.

Literature Links
Eats Poems. *Arnold Adolf. New York: Lothrop, Lee and Shepard Books, 1979. This is a mouth-watering collection of food poems to savor.*

How to Eat a Poem and Other Morsels. *Rose Agree. New York: Pantheon Books, 1983. More poems about food and eating.*

Sam's Sandwich. *David Pelham. New York: Dutton Children's Books, 1990. Humorous quatrains reveal how Sam's sister wants his sandwich! Sam adds surprises to the sandwich which is cleverly created through the pages of the book.*

"A Vote for Vanilla" by Eve Merriam in **It Doesn't Always Have to Rhyme**, *illustrated by Malcolm Sooner, Atheneum, 1972.*

"Chocolate Cake" by Nina Payne in **All the Day Long**, *illustrated by Laurel Schindelman. New York: Atheneum, 1973.*

Where the Sidewalk Ends. *Shel Silverstein, New York: Harper & Row, 1974. This rich resource is loaded with poems that will remind you and your students that food is an experience for all the senses!*

40. Punctuation Pals

Materials
- tagboard
- construction paper
- yarn, buttons, any other collage materials
- glue

Circle Time Talk
Look through some of your students' favorite big books and find one that has at least one exclamation mark, question mark, a set of quotation marks and, of course, a period. Read through the story once with your class for the pleasure of it. Read through it again, being certain that the inflection in your voice communicates the type of sentence you are reading. Point out the punctuation marks. Explain that they are good "pals" because they tell us exactly how to read and understand a story. And that's important!

Activity
1. Make a large tagboard pattern of punctuation marks. Invite the students to trace them on construction paper and cut them out. Encourage them to use their imaginations to give their "punctuation pals" a personality. Have them use buttons and yarn to add to their creations.

2. Print sentences on the board and have students come up and place the appropriate mark of punctuation at the end. Provide magnets with clips to hold the punctuation pals in place.

3. Give the punctuation pals back to the students. Read a classroom favorite, like the two stories listed in the Literature Links and at the end of each sentence have the students hold up the appropriate mark of punctuation.

Extension Activities
- On the back of the punctuation pals, have the students tell the kind of punctuation mark it is and write a sentence using that punctuation mark. You can also let them know the names of the kinds of sentences the punctuation mark makes. For example, a period at the end of the sentence tells us that it could be a command or a telling sentence.

- This activity can be adapted for your prereaders. Follow the same Circle Time Talk procedure and #1 of the Activity directions. However, instead of writing sentences on the chalkboard for students to read and identify, recite a sentence to your students and ask them "What kind of sentence is this? A telling sentence? An exclamation? A question?" Ask your students to then hold the correct punctuation pal in the air.

Literature Links
Green Eggs and Ham. *Theodore S. Geisel. New York: Random House, Inc., 1960. This book provides different punctuation marks as examples of this skill.*

Spot Goes to the Circus. *Eric Hill. New York: Putnam's Sons, 1986. This is an enjoyable book about a dog's adventure at the circus that would be a good source for teaching punctuation skills.*

41. It's Easy as ABC

Materials
- premade alphabet letters at least 9" (22.86 cm)
- any alphabet song

Circle Time Talk

Here is a fun way to reinforce letter recognition skills. Read one of the books from the Literature Links suggestions. Point out to the students which letters have straight lines and curved lines. Also notice which letters have no straight lines at all! Ask children to trace the first letter in their own name in the air on their "magic chalkboards." Sing the alphabet song. When singing, allow the children to clap once when they hear the letter of their first name.

Activity

1. Play an alphabet song. Perhaps "Marching Around the Alphabet" by Hap Palmer. Ask students to listen especially for the letter of their first names.

2. Place your alphabet letters randomly in a circle. March around the alphabet following the song. Place letters with straight lines in one pile. Place the letters with curved lines in another. Make another pile for letters that have both straight and curved lines. Allow the children to touch and examine the letters.

3. For older children, you can play Musical Alphabet. Play and stop the song every few seconds. When the music stops, the children will pick up the closest letter and name a noun, verb, etc., that begins with that letter.

Extension Activities

- Encourage the children to use their bodies to form certain letters. Put children into groups of three. Assign a letter to each group. Allow enough time for children to cooperate with one another to figure out how to make that particular letter.

- Try using clay, sand, paint, cotton, macaroni, shaving cream, flavored gelatin, etc., to create different letters of the alphabet. Share and display these creative alphabet works!

Literature Links

Learning the letters of the alphabet can be fun when observing the artistic and creative ways they are presented in the following books.

The ABC Bunny.
Wanda Gag. New York: Coward, 1933.

Brian Wildsmith's ABC. *Brian Wildsmith. New York: Watts, 1962.*

ABC: An Alphabet Book. *Thomas Matthiesen. New York: Grossett and Dunlop, Inc., 1981.*

42. Walk a Story

Materials
- drawing paper
- crayons
- masking tape
- laminator or clear self-adhesive paper

Circle Time Talk
Your students will never forget reading this story! Take a vote with the class to select their favorite story. When counting votes to determine the winner, use words like *most* and *least*. Read the story to the class. Review skills such as author, title page, beginning, middle and end. Explain that tomorrow they will create this story in a very special way.

Activity

1. Prepare the text of the class's favorite story on drawing paper (including the cover and title page). The text should be placed on the paper as it is in the book. Don't forget to number the pages!

2. Distribute prepared pages for the children to illustrate.

3. Lay the pages down and tape the pages together in order. Laminate or use clear self-adhesive paper over the entire story.

4. Now, take your shoes off, take a walk and read the story together.

Extension Activities
- Have children hop, crawl, sit, stand, etc., to different parts of the story. Examples: "Jose, please stand where the story begins." "Kristy, sit on the title page."

- Have prepared word cards with words like *cover, title page, author, beginning, middle* and *end*. Read the word cards together. Choose volunteers to place these cards identifying the correct parts of the story.

Literature Links
Walking these stories would be an experience children would not soon forget . . . a real treat for the feet!

Chicken Soup with Rice. *Maurice Sendak. New York: Harper, 1962.*

If You Give a Mouse a Cookie. *Laura Numeroff. New York: Harper, 1985.*

Over in the Meadow. *Olive Wadsworth. New York: Viking, 1985.*

43. Compound Connection

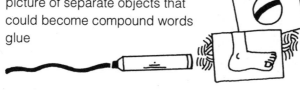

Materials

- large index cards
- yarn
- marker
- hole punch
- picture of separate objects that could become compound words
- glue

Circle Time Talk

Arrange students in a circle. Review compound words with students. Have pictures, objects or drawings available. Choose two pictures that could become a compound, such as a "foot" and a "ball." Distribute pictures to students. Choose one student to stand holding his or her picture. If a classmate has a picture that matches to make a compound, he or she then stands. The class then judges if it makes a "compound connection." If it does, they sit together in the circle and continue to play the game.

Compound Words

foot/ball
chalk/board
base/ball
dog/house
toe/nail
cup/cake
pony/tail
ear/ring
cat/fish

Activity

1. Prepare this game by writing words on large index cards that, with other words on other cards, make compound words. Punch two holes in the index card and attach yarn to the cards.

2. Pass out "word necklaces" and have students wear them. Students then walk silently around the room trying to find their compound connection.

3. After they have found their partners, they sit in a designated area until all have completed the game. Then partners stand and recite their compound words.

4. Record the compounds on a chart. Read the words again for review.

Extension Activities

- Use this game to connect other words. For example: join root words with prefixes or suffixes, antonyms with synonyms, rhyming word partners.

- Prereaders can play the Compound Connection game using pictures instead of words.

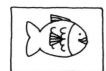 

Literature Links

Have students cite compound words from the books below.

Good-Bye, Arnold!
Patricia K. Roche. New York: Dial Press, 1979. Webster learns to value his brother after spending time alone.

In Any Treehouse.
Alice Schertle. New York: Lothrop, Lee and Shephard, 1983. A boy finds a home away from home in his tree house.

44. Bag a Book

Materials
- large brown shopping bags
- crayons or colored pencils

Circle Time Talk
Discuss with students a favorite book they have read recently. What was their favorite part of the story? Who was the author? Where did it take place? Who were the characters in the story?

Activity
1. Ask students to bring in their favorite books. Distribute large brown bags to the students. On the front of the bag, have them write the name and author of the book, and draw a favorite scene from the story. On the right side of the bag, have students write a brief summary. On the left side have them rate the book from one to four stars (four being the best!), and write a comment for the rationale of this rating. On the back of the bag, the students can write their names, school address and grade.

2. When completed, your students can share "Bag a Book" reports orally and display them in the corridors or in the media/library center.

Extension Activities
- Give these completed bags to a local grocery store, asking that they distribute them to families with school-age children.

- Have students write a request on the bag for a "reader's response" which can be sent to their school.

- Send a note home to parents encouraging them to put a few different books in a bag every week that can be decorated at home. Each night one can be chosen for family "story time."

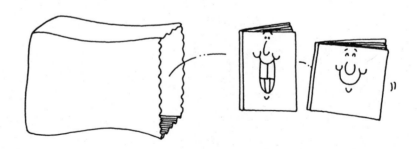

Literature Links
Petunia. *Roger Duvoisin. New York: Knopf, 1950. Petunia the goose finds a book believing it will make her wise. A series of misadventures with her barnyard friends follows.*

Andy and the Lion. *James Daugherty. Viking, 1938. Andy reads a book about lions and finally finds one with a thorn in its paw. Andy meets the escaped lion again at the circus but recognizes him and thereby saves the audience.*

Broderick. *Edward Ormondroyd. New York: Houghton Mifflin, 1984. Broderick the mouse, discovers the purpose of books and changes the meaning of his life.*

45. Words of Fortune

Materials
- chalkboard
- eraser and chalk

Circle Time Talk
Review the rules of your own version of the game Hangman. Tell students they are going to guess a vocabulary or spelling word, and the winner will receive a small prize. Put them in groups of three or four.

Activity

1. Have one group of students come to the chalkboard. Put as many lines on the board as there are letters in the chosen review word.
   Example: __ __ __ __ __ __ *(summer)*

2. Ask the first student in the group to guess a letter. If that letter is in the chosen word, write it on the line where it appears.
   Example: __ __ __ __ e __
   If that letter is used in the word, the student may guess another letter.

3. If the letter is not used in the word, the letter can be written to the side of the board under the heading "Not Used."
   Example: <u>Not Used</u> __ __ __ __ e __
   j
   b

4. Then the next student gets a chance to guess a letter. The student who guesses a correct letter always has a chance to guess the word when it is his or her turn.

5. If students guess aloud when it is not their turn, they miss their chance.

Extension Activities
- Students can also be asked to spell the entire word, define it or use it in a sentence.

- Vocabulary in other content areas can be chosen for the game.

Literature Links
These books will provide other ideas for fun with word games.

Puzzles and Quizzles. *Helen Fletcher. New York: Abelard-Schuman, Abel, 1973.*

The Magic of Words. *Chicago: Field Enterprises Educational Corporation, Co., 1975.*

46. Colors of the Week

Materials

- books on color
  (see Literature Links)
- sponges
- various colors of
  tempera or watercolor paints
- apples
- art paper
- food coloring, water
- graph paper
- acrylic cutting board
- brayer

- hard-boiled eggs
- pudding
- flavored gelatin
- construction paper
- colored blocks or beads
- string
- green cotton balls
- 35mm film canisters
- moving eyes (can be
  purchased in a craft shop)
- blue liquid tempera paint

Literature Links

The various suggested books cite different colors. Select ones you will be focusing on during the "colorful" weeks ahead.

The Black Cat. *Allan Ahlberg. New York: Greenwillow, 1990.*

Three Gold Pieces. *Aliki. New York: Pantheon Books, 1967.*

Yellow Ball. *Molly Garrett Bang. New York: Morrow, 1991.*

The Prince and the Pink Blanket. *Barbara Brenner. New York: Four Winds Press, 1980.*

Yellow Umbrella. *Henrik Drescher. New York: Bradbury, 1987.*

A Rainbow of My Own. *Don Freeman. New York: Viking Press, 1966.*

The Blue Bird. *Fiona French. New York: Henry Z. Walch, 1972.*

Little Red Hen. *Paul Galdone. Boston: Houghton Mifflin, 1973.*

Little Red Riding Hood. *Trina Schart Hyman. New York: Holiday House, 1983.*

Brown Cow Farm: A Counting Book. *Dahlov Ipcar. New York: Doubleday, 1959.*

Circle Time Talk

Colors are discovered in everything a child sees. Knowing the names and what they are is important to the young learner. Discuss what the world would be like if everything was the same color. Discuss how color makes the world exciting and different.

Activities

1. Each week focus on a particular color. Use the suggested books, songs and poems to help introduce and reinforce certain colors.

2. Each Monday read a story that discusses many or all of the colors you are choosing to review or introduce. Display the name of the color of the week in large letters several places throughout the classroom. By the end of the week your students will know how to read the name of the color of the week.

3. Each Friday have children wear the color of the week.

4. Here are suggested activities to use with certain colors:

Red:
   a. Discuss red as a primary color.
   b. Find things in the room that are red. Count items; then start a graph called "The Colors in Our Room." Keep track each week of the number of items in the graph. Talk about the color that is found most and least in the classroom. For example: How many more yellow items are there than green?
   c. Make an apple print using real apples or sponges cut into apple shapes.
   d. Make red gelatin shapes.

TLC10001 Copyright © Teaching & Learning Company, Carthage, IL 62321

Blue:
    a. Discuss blue as a primary color.
    b. Graph the number of blue items found in the classroom.
    c. Make blueberry pancakes.
    d. Do blue monoprints with your students. Squeeze blue tempera paint onto an acrylic cutting board. Roll it with an ink brayer until it is fairly even. Your students will draw their pictures into the surface of the wet tempera. Place a piece of paper on top of the paint. Rub it gently; then carefully lift it and hang it to dry.

Yellow:
    a. Discuss yellow as a primary color.
    b. Graph the number of yellow items found in the classroom.
    c. Easel paint or finger paint using yellow.
    d. Share lemonade and bananas as a snack.

Green:
    a. Graph the number of green items found in the classroom.
    b. Review how green can be made from blue and yellow.
    c. Create Oscar the Grouch. Collect 35mm film canisters. Glue a green cotton ball inside the canister so that the head is popping out. Then glue the top of the canister to make it look like the garbage can is open. Add moving eyes and a nose.
    d. Make green eggs and ham!
    e. Mix paint or food coloring and water (a little blue, a little yellow).

5. Other activities to do with different colors:
    a. Color hard-boiled eggs.
    b. Make pudding. (Add food coloring to vanilla or banana flavors.)

    c. Go outside and find a certain color.
    d. Rip Art—Give each child a certain color of construction paper. Rip paper into designs. Glue on another piece of construction paper.
    e. String Paint—Use 18" (45.72 cm) piece of string. Dip string into paint except for the ends. Fold art paper over the string and pull string to make designs.
    f. Sort blocks or beads using various colors.
    g. Memorize "color" songs or poems. Examples: "Baa Baa Black Sheep," "Purple Cow," "What Is Pink?" by Christian Rosetti.

Extension Activities

• Make a mobile of different colored objects. Hang them around the room.

• Write a cheer for colors.

• Make a classroom chart entitled "Our Favorite Colors." Discuss chart as you have done for the culminating activity for items around the room.

• Twister™, anyone?

47. For Keat's Sake

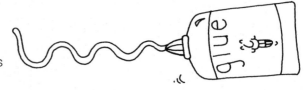

Materials
- large leaf pattern
- large flower pattern
- construction paper
- glue and scissors
- writing paper and pencils

Ezra Jack Keats was born in Brooklyn, New York, on March 11, 1916. He was educated at Thomas Jefferson High School in Brooklyn. Keats served in the United States Army Air Corps during World War II. He was a muralist for the Works Progress Administration in the 1930s and then became a freelance commercial artist. He received the American Library Association Caldecott Medal in 1963, the Boston Globe-Horn Book Award for illustration in 1970 and the University of Southern Mississippi Award in 1980. Ezra Jack Keats died on May 6, 1983.

Circle Time Talk

Focusing on a single favorite author or illustrator is a wonderful way to stimulate a love of reading. Circle time for the duration of this activity will be spent reading the works of your chosen author or illustrator.

Activity

1. Make a wall display saying "Growing and Learning in the Garden of Ezra Jack Keats." Make various sized 3' to 6' (.9144 to 1.8288 m) flower stems. At the top of each stem will be a flower with the name of a Keats' book. Add details to the wall like paper butterflies and grass.

2. Introduce the students to Ezra Jack Keats. Explain to them that they will be learning three parts of stories called "character, setting and main idea." Read the various stories of Keats, one each day. Help students become familiar with the three parts of each story.

3. Students will write this information on writing paper: title, author's name, names of characters, setting and main idea. Choose certain students to recopy their original work on a precut leaf-shaped piece of writing paper. Glue the writing paper on a precut leaf-shaped piece of construction paper and add it to a stem on the wall. Each child will have work represented for various books.

Extension Activities

- Write a letter to an author. They should include in their letters which book they liked best, their favorite character and why.

- This activity can be easily adapted to an illustrator. Students who are prewriters can draw a picture that will be added to the wall display.

48. Birthday Parties for Books

Materials

- various storybooks from class library
- party hats, noisemakers
- balloons, streamers
- word cards that name: cover, title page, dedication page, author, illustrator
- prepared snacks
- poster board
- crayons, markers

Circle Time Talk

Everyone enjoys celebrating birthdays, so why not celebrate a book's birthday? When a new age-appropriate book becomes available in print, have a party! Discuss with your students their experiences at birthday parties. Share what games were played, who was there and what types of treats were served.

Share with students that children's books are always being printed. Show children copyright pages from books and determine the dates that are from the past and present. Get the children excited about sharing the "birth" of a newly printed book. Choose a book from the Literature Links section and celebrate!

Activity

1. Tell the children that books are not only made up of stories, but they also have a cover, a title page, a dedication page, an author and an illustrator. Show these pages from the new book.

2. Read a selected story wearing party hats with balloons scattered about the room. Discuss how they enjoyed the story, their favorite parts, etc.

3. Read and distribute word cards. Show (again) different parts of the new book. Children should stand if they have the word card that matches the book part being shown.

4. Create snacks and games related to the book. Engage class parents to help in the preparation of snacks.

5. Make bookmarks from poster board as party favors. Include title, author and a picture of a character or favorite part.

Extension Activities

- Find out the author's birthday. Sing "Happy Birthday" when his or her birthday arrives. Read the story again on that day.

- Design T-shirts or pillowcases about the book using puffy paints or fabric crayons.

- Learn "Happy Birthday" in sign language.

Literature Links
Ten Little Bunnies.

Nurit Karlin. New York: Simon & Schuster, 1994. This funny counting book will help children learn the numbers 1 through 10. Birthday party activities such as the Bunny Hop, telling knock-knock jokes and making puns can be gleaned from this story.

The Dumb Bunnies.

Sue Denim. New York: The Blue Sky Press, 1994. This hilariously funny book tells the story of three really dumb bunnies and all their really dumb stunts. Did you ever put ketchup on watermelon, drink potato chips or dance a merry dance? Maybe you will want to try at your celebration.

49. Reading Rangers Creative Center

Materials
- books used during sharing or Circle Time Talk
- big books, class and individually authored books, songs, poems, chants (on chart paper), trade books
- easel and pointer
- display racks or shelves
- tape recorder and recorded stories
- rocking chair
- rugs, pillows or cushions
- table and chairs
- headphones
- stuffed animals
- magazines
- flannel board

Circle Time Talk
Pupil-directed activities allow students to take control of their learning. Reading (one part of the language process) engagement activities gets children excited and eager to practice what they are learning. Reinforce rules that pertain to this activity center.

Activity
Your students can use the reading center in the following ways:

1. Form a group around the book easel while one student acts as the leader using the pointer, as the other children read along.
2. Sit around a table and enjoy listening and reading along to a taped book with a tape recorder and headphones.
3. Sit in a rocking chair reading an old favorite or a new story with a furry friend.
4. Take a walk to each poem or chant written on chart paper. Recite the poem or chant; then walk to the next chart and repeat the process.
5. Pull up a rug and a story with your buddy, friend or teacher.
6. Spy for new books on the display racks.
7. Search for a book by your favorite author. Read the book with expression—just like the author would read it.
8. Enjoy a flannel board story.
9. Classify books into schemes, alphabetically, by author, according to size, etc.
10. Read, read, read!

Praise children for excellent work.

Extension Activities
- Invite an author, parent or principal to read and share a story with the class. This makes sharing very special.

- Take a trip to the library. Discuss with parents the importance of children having a library card. If students do not have a card, let parents prearrange for their child to receive one on the class trip.

- Establish a DEAR (Drop Everything And Read) or SSR (Sustained Silent Reading) time in class.

Literature Links
These fun-loving stories will enchant your young readers.

Curious George.
H.A. Rey. Boston: Houghton Mifflin, 1973.

Frederick. *Leo Lionni. New York: Pantheon, 1966.*

Harry the Dirty Dog.
Gene Zion. New York: Harper, 1976.

50. Poetry Box

Materials

- small empty boxes such as shoe boxes or gift boxes
- poetry books
- glue, scissors
- writing paper, pencils
- construction paper

Circle Time Talk

Gather the students together and have poetry books available for them to read. Encourage them to find favorite ones to share with their classmates. Which ones did they choose? Who are the poets? Why did they single out these particular poems?

Activity

1. Provide the students with empty boxes, or ask them to bring boxes to school for an assignment. Direct students to choose a favorite poem and write it on a piece of paper. Next they are to cover the inside of the box with construction paper and glue the poem to the colored paper. They then can find pictures from magazines to complement the poem and glue them on the inside of the box also. The lid of the box can also be covered with construction paper, and students can write the name and author of the poem here. The lid can be attached to the back of the opened box for display.

2. Students can share creative poetry boxes with each other and read aloud their favorite verses.

3. Display poetry boxes in the media/library center for all to enjoy. Delight parents at an Open House or PTA meeting.

Extension Activities

- Have students memorize a poem to recite in class.

- Act out a poem.

- Play instrumental music during poetry recitation.

- Recite a poem in unison or in parts.

- Read poetry to your class every day. Choose one appropriate to the mood of the day or for incorporation into another subject area.

- Have a puppet recite a poem.

- Encourage students to share poetry with their parents and grandparents.

Literature Links

The Sky Is Full of Song. *Lee Bennett Hopkins. New York: Harper Junior Books, 1983. Thirty-eight short seasonal poems are included by outstanding poets.*

Listen, Children, Listen: An Anthology of Poems for the Very Young. *Edited by Myra C. Livingston. New York: Harcourt, 1972. A wonderful collection of child-centered poetry to read to your students is available in this book.*

Surprises. *Edited by Lee Bennett Hopkins. New York: Harper Junior Books, 1984. Fun-filled and imaginative poems dealing with boats, trains, planes, rain, sun, snow and good-night feelings.*

Where the Sidewalk Ends. *Shel Silverstein. New York: Harper & Row, 1974. A poetry book students can't put down and always choose to read over and over.*

51. Pocket Chart Creative Center

Materials
- various pocket charts
- index cards
- sentence strips
- classification cards of colors, shapes, numbers, etc.

Circle Time Talk
Using pocket charts will help you reinforce many skills you are teaching in the classroom. Individuals or groups of children can use these materials to help gain mastery over skills such as letter writing, letter or word recognition, or alphabetizing. Explain the materials and their use for this center. Review rules as well.

Activities
Pocket charts can be used for the following:

1. Prepare index cards or sentence strips with words labeled *Date, Opening, Body/Message, Closing* and *Signature/Name*. Children can place these word cards on the chart to represent the correct way a letter is written.
2. Classify numbers, shapes, short or long vowel sounds, or animals into appropriately labeled pockets.
3. Laminate and cut up comic strips. Children can put strips in order using wall chart.
4. Sequence pictures by size.
5. Use a wall chart to classify "hard" and "soft" *th* digraph.
6. Label pockets with months of the year; then place seasonal pictures in the correct pockets. For example, a picture of a heart would be placed in the February pocket.
7. Pair up antonyms: dull, sharp; quiet, noisy; young, old; on, off; good, bad; thin, fat; first, last; yes, no; etc.
8. Children can make their own task cards to write words using a word family you may be learning: –ack, –eam, –ink, –op, –at, –own, –unk, –an, –eat or blends they are learning: bl, tr, sp, gl, dr, fr, st, sl.
9. Use pocket chart to categorize words with 1, 2, 3 or 4 syllables.
10. Classify "hard" and "soft" *C* words. Hard: candy, cup, candle, car, camel, clap, crow, clock. Soft: cigar, cent, fence, nice, circle, mice, circus, face.

Extension Activities
- Create a pocket chart for Creative Centers! Assign a pocket for each center in your classroom. On the pocket specify the name of the center and the number of children allowed to use that particular center at one time. Make students name tags to fit into the pockets for the teacher or student to make a center selection.

- Create a pocket chart for yourself. Keep your supplies, such as index cards, glue, paper clips, rubber bands, etc., at your fingertips.

Literature Links
Cinderella. *Marcia Brown. New York: Charles Scribner's Sons, 1954. "Smile" when you hear the "soft" C in this favorite fairy tale of a wicked stepmother, mean stepsisters and a prince.*

Curious George.
H.A. Rey. Boston: Houghton Mifflin, 1973. "Clap" when you hear the "hard" C in this funny story of a mischievous monkey and his friend.

Pocket Chart Resource Book.
Susan Ketch. North Carolina: Carson-Dellosa Publishing Co., 1991.

52. In the Mood

Materials
- colored electrical tape (blue, red, black, yellow, green)

Circle Time Talk
This activity will allow children to develop an understanding of characters' feelings and moods in a story. Ask the children what makes them angry, happy, sad, etc., and why. Sing "If You're Happy and You Know It." Replace *Happy* with other words that describe feelings. This activity works best with smaller groups.

Activity

1. Create four squares on the floor with black tape. Each square should be large enough for a least six children to stand in.

2. On the inside of each square, create shapes using different colored tape. Make a face inside each shape with tape that describes a different feeling.
   Example: yellow — happy
   blue — sad
   green — scared
   red — angry

3. Choose a story from Literature Links or another story that deals with feelings. Tell the children that they will hear a story in which events take place to make the main character feel a certain way.

4. Tell the children that they should listen carefully to the story. When the teacher stops the story to ask how the main character is feeling, they are to stand in the appropriate square.

5. Discuss with the children why they are standing in the square with the blue, sad, triangle face (or whatever square they have chosen to stand in). Discuss the events that made the character feel that way.

Extension Activities

- For a clearer assessment of a child's understanding of cause and effect, give children a blank piece of drawing paper folded into fourths. Read a short story, stopping four times to allow the children to draw a face that describes the way the character is feeling at that time in the story. Discuss their choices. Older students can write why the character's mood changed.

- Act out the situations in a story where the character's moods change. Discuss times in life when that has happened to you.

Literature Links
Daddy Is a Monster. *John Steptoe. New York: Lippincott, 1980. Family tension and anger are real feelings. See how a brother and sister deal with their family conflict.*

Crow Boy. *Taro Yashima. New York: Viking Press, 1955. A Japanese boy finally gets a new nickname after many years of being called "Tiny Boy." Discover his feelings and change of mood.*

Sleeping Ugly. *Jane Yolen. New York: Coward, McCann, 1981. How would you feel if you lost a prince to a homely but nice girl. Princess Miserella shares many feelings about her experience.*

Strega Nona. *Tomie de Paola. Englewood Cliffs: Prentice Hall, 1975. Big Anthony discovers the magic powers of Strega Nona's pasta pot. His experiences will make you laugh, but does it make Big Anthony happy?*

53. Picture Prediction Hang-Up

Materials

- clothesline
- clothespins
- story cards (text for readers, illustrations for prereaders)

Circle Time Talk

The story cards needed for this activity can be adapted from a published story (see Literature Links), or you can create a simple story. The main idea is for the children to be able to predict what might happen next in a story. Read the following story to your students.

Two girls are riding their bikes on the street. There is a pothole in the ground. One of the girls doesn't see the pothole, and she's headed straight for it. What might happen to her?

Activity

1. Hang the story cards out of order on the clothesline. Allow the children to look at and observe these pictures for a few moments.

2. Have a volunteer go forward and rearrange the story two cards at a time.

3. Stop and discuss the way in which the story is being rearranged. Continually ask "What do you think will happen next?" as each child takes his or her turn.

4. Continue step 3 until the story pictures are in their proper places. With your students, retell the story from beginning to end.

Extension Activities

- This activity can be used to help review alphabetical order. Make two sets of alphabet cards (upper or lowercase). Arrange class into two teams. The first team to put cards in ABC order is the winner!

- Students can dramatize the "clothesline story." Have volunteers stand under a picture hanging on the clothesline. They will tell and act out that part of the story. When they finish they will immediately say "and then." They will "freeze" and the next person in line will continue the story. This continues until the last picture card is acted out and told, and the student says, "The end." All students will "unfreeze" and take a bow for a terrific performance!

Literature Links

The following are fun, exciting, books perfect for any clothesline story.

The Three Little Pigs. *Paul Galdone. San Francisco: Seabury Press, 1970.*

Mary Had a Little Lamb. *Tomie de Paola. New York: Holiday Press, 1984.*

Jack and the Beanstalk. *Paul Galdone. New York: Clarion, 1982.*

The Gingerbread Boy. *Ed Arno. New York: Scholastic, 1975.*

54. On the Loose with Mother Goose

Materials

- 12" x 36" (.30 x .91 m) butcher paper
- pencils, crayons
- construction paper
- sentence strips (strips of paper 2" [5.08 cm] high by 20" [50.8 cm] long)
- glue
- pocket chart

Circle Time Talk

Share some nursery rhymes with the children using a selection from Literature Links or another book of your choice. Encourage students to join in and recite their favorites from memory.

Activity

1. Prepare for this activity by choosing a nursery rhyme and printing each line on a sentence strip.

2. Have students read the Mother Goose rhyming lines from the chart. Then distribute sentence strips to volunteers who will come forward to put the rhyme in sequential order on the chalkboard ledge or in the pocket chart.

3. Read the poem when the sentence strips have been put in sequential order. Have volunteers try to recite it from memory.

Extension Activities

- Distribute paper and crayons to students and assist them in making a classroom book (directions below). Have them choose a nursery rhyme, and write a different verse on each page according to correct sequential order. Use construction paper and crayons to illustrate it.

- Have students write a contemporary nursery rhyme. Example:

  Humpty Dumpty went to the mall.
  Humpty Dumpty had a great fall.
  All of the shoppers who were walking by,
  Helped Humpty when he started to cry!

Book Directions #1

1. For each book, choose as many pieces of poster board as there are pages of the story. On each page, use crayons to draw and write about the scene, or cut out and glue pictures from a magazine.

2. Create a cover which includes the title and student's name. Punch three holes in the sides of each page and the cover.

3. Use yarn, string or ribbon to lace sheets together.

Book Directions #2

Fold a 1' x 3' (.30 x .91 m) sheet of butcher paper in half and then into equal parts. A front and back cover can be made from construction paper.

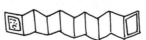

Literature Links

These nursery rhymes are sure to delight your class!

The Mother Goose Treasury. *Raymond Briggs. New York: Coward, McCann & Geoghegan, Inc., 1966.*

Mother Goose: A Collection of Nursery Rhymes. *Brian Wildsmith. New York: Franklin Watts, Inc., 1964.*

55. Mapping Mural

Materials
- large paper for mural
- masking tape
- crayons, felt-tip markers
- construction paper
- scissors
- overhead projector

Circle Time Talk
Bring a road map to the circle. Ask your students if they know what it is. Have their parents ever used a map when traveling? How did it help them? Where were they going? Explain to students that a story map helps them to sequence events and put them in order from the beginning of the story to the end of the story.

Activity
1. On an overhead projector, use colored felt-tip markers to write a simple form for a story map.

2. Read one of the selections from Literature Links or another classroom favorite and have student volunteers fill in the necessary information. *The Three Bears* story map might read as follows:

> Title
> Characters
> Setting
> Conflict
> Event 1
> Event 2
> Event 3
> Conclusion

Title	The Three Bears
Characters	Goldilocks, the Three Bears
Setting	House in the forest
Conflict	Bears disturbed by an intruder
Event 1	Bears go for a walk
Event 2	Goldilocks enters house, eats porridges, breaks chair, sleeps in beds
Event 3	Bears return while Goldilocks sleeps
Conclusion	Bears scare Goldilocks from their home

Extension Activities
- Before this activity, divide the story into four to six sequential events that your students will be able to illustrate. Divide your students into as many groups as you have events. Explain that they are going to create a story mural. Distribute construction paper, crayons and scissors and let them go to work. After the illustrations are complete, talk about which picture should go first on the wall, second, etc. This activity will also reinforce left to right directionality.

- Volunteers can retell the story in their own words following the events pictured in the mural.

Literature Links
These books would be appropriate to read before the mapping mural activities.

The Three Bears.
Paul Galdone. San Francisco: Seabury Press, 1973. A colorful tale of one of the best-loved children's stories.

The Biggest Bear.
Lynd Ward. Boston: Houghton, 1972. Johnny brings home a cute bear cub that alarms neighbors by its constant growth.

56. Play Day

Materials
- books of plays
- props for plays
- chalkboard, chalk
- overhead projector
- writing paper, pencils

Circle Time Talk
Ask students if they have ever seen a play or participated in one. Have students share their experiences. What characters did they see in the play or portray? What props were used?

Activity

1. Choose one of the selections from Literature Links or another book of your choice that contains plays for children. Ask for volunteers, and distribute copies of the play to the students with their parts highlighted. Provide the necessary props and give them practice time. Explain to the volunteers that they will read the lines a few times and try to act out their parts as best they can in loud, clear voices.

2. Students can draw on the chalkboard to provide a simple background setting for their play or draw different scenes on the overhead projector.

3. Speak to the rest of the class about audience behavior, such as when they should listen, when they should applaud, how they should focus on the play and not on distracting noises.

Extension Activity
- Encourage students to work with a partner or group to write their own plays. Students can base their play on a story they have read in class or one they have heard during story time.

Literature Links
The following selections are short, lively plays with easy material for young children.

Short Plays for Children. Helen Miller. Boston: Plays, Inc., 1960.

First Plays for Children. Helen Miller. Boston: Plays, Inc., 1960.

Small Plays for Special Days. Sue Alexander. New York: Houghton Mifflin, 1977.

Humorous Monologues. Marcia Bolton. New York: Sterling Co., Inc., 1989.

Little Plays for Little Players. Sylvia Kamerman. Boston: Plays, Inc., 1952.

57. Spin a Story

Materials
- paper plates (2 for each student)
- brad clips
- scissors
- crayons or markers
- rulers
- stapler
- construction paper
- writing paper

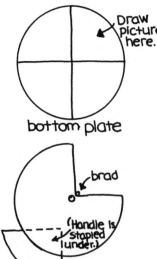

Circle Time Talk
After the class completes this activity as a whole, place the above stated materials in the Reading Center for children to do on their own. Share a short story or nursery rhyme with the class. Then review what happened first, next, then and last. Explain to the class the importance of sequence in a story. This activity will help them visualize that.

Activity
1. Supply each student with two paper plates, ruler, brad clip, writing and construction paper.

2. Help children write the sequence of the shared story or rhyme. For each sequence step, a new line must be started. You may want to have this prepared for the younger students. Cut paper equal size; then set aside.

Jack and Jill went up the hill	to fetch a pail of water.	Jack fell down and broke his crown,	and Jill came tumbling after.

3. Take a piece of construction paper, cut to be the same size as the writing paper. (You may want to also have this prepared to save time.) Write the title and author of the story or rhyme on paper to act as a cover. Three-hole punch the pages and tie them together with yarn. Set aside with story/rhyme.

4. Divide one paper plate in fourths using the black crayon or marker and a ruler.

5. Draw pictures in each section that correspond to each page of story or rhyme from step 2.

6. Place the other plate on top and insert the brad through both plates. Cut a window in the top plate. Use the lines on the underneath plate as a guide.

7. Staple the part of the plate which was cut for the window under the first plate to help hold while turning the back plate.

8. Staple the written story to the top plate. Spin the back plate and read the story or rhyme.

9. When you place your spin-a-stories in your reading center, store them in a Ziploc™ bag with the book you created in steps 3 and 4.

Literature Links
Chinese Mother Goose Rhymes.

Robert Wyndham. New York: Philomel, 1982. Edward Young illustrates this book in calligraphy. The pages are filled with Chinese rhymes and riddles which have been retold to the young for hundreds of years.

The Sky Is Full of Song. *Lee Bennett Hopkins. New York: Harper Junior Books, 1983. Many outstanding poets are recognized in this book of 38 short poems. These poems help visualize the scenes of each season. Spin a poem and enjoy.*

Heckedy Peg. *Audrey Wood. New York: Harcourt, 1987. A mother of seven outsmarts a witch who has captured and bewitched her children. Spin this story or create a spin-off. Either way, it's fun.*

Extension Activities

- Older students can divide plates into eighths (making the window smaller) and make their story longer with more detail. Of course, they can make up their own story or rhyme to share with the class.

- Spin a Vowel. Use the same steps as in Activity except for making the window. Divide bottom plate into as many sections as needed. Draw pictures and write the medial vowel sound above it.

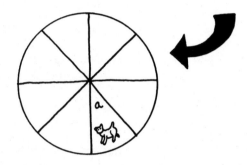

Cut the window on the top plate like this:

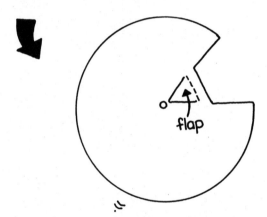

The pictures should be seen through the cut. The vowel should be covered until the student bends the flap to reveal the vowel sound. The bottom plate can be replaced with beginning or ending sounds.

(finished example)

58. Transparent Stories

Materials
- overhead projector
- transparencies
- markers
- storybook
- paper bag or wrapping paper
- chalkboard, chalk

Circle Time Talk
Take a break! Ask a volunteer to choose a storybook to read to the class. Make sure the student has had a chance to practice reading at home before he or she reads it to the class. Emergent readers will need your help for this activity.

Activity
1. Ask your student reader to cover the storybook with a paper bag or wrapping paper. During recess ask the student to read the story to you for extra practice.

2. List the characters, setting, etc., on the board. Allow the student reader to explain each item.

3. Gather students around the "author's chair." The reader will give the title and author of the story. The reader reads the story to the class without showing the illustrations.

4. After the story is read, students will get into groups and draw illustrations on transparency material they think would go with the story. One group draws what happened first, another group draws what happened next and so on.

5. Read the story again using transparency illustrations.

6. Unwrap the book. Show the cover and illustrations. Read the story a third time.

7. Talk about the students' illustrations and the original illustrations.

Extension Activities
- Select a poem to read to the class. Invite the children to work in groups to draw an illustration (on a transparency) fitting the words expressed in the poem. To help students visualize the illustration, allow them to close their eyes during the recitation. Choose a reader in each group to recite the poem as the illustration is being shown on the overhead.

- Save the transparencies in a file folder. Label folder with title and author. At a later date, put this story in the overhead projector center. Children can use the illustrations to retell or make up their own stories.

Literature Links
In the Night Kitchen. *Maurice Sendak. New York: Harper & Row, 1970. This delightful dream fantasy book illustrates a child's wild imagination. Students will enjoy creating wild, imaginative illustrations.*

Arthur's Eyes. *Marc Brown. Boston: Little Brown, 1979. Arthur deals with the difficulty of owning a pair of glasses. This common event will allow students to visualize personal illustrations easily.*

The Cut-Ups Cut Loose. *James Marshall. New York: Puffin, 1989. Two boys are the neighborhood and school clowns. Students will enjoy listening to their antics in combating Mr. Spurgle (the school principal) with rubber snakes and spit balls. Imagine the illustrations your students will produce!*

59. Author Unknown (Not Any More!)

Materials
- variety of books written by the same author
- butcher paper
- index cards or blank paper (same size)
- masking tape
- pencils or crayons
- black marker
- yardstick

Circle Time Talk

Encourage your students to get to know the authors behind all the wonderful stories they hear. Choose an author to study for your students to complete this activity. The more familiar children become with age-appropriate literature, the more they'll know about various authors. Soon *your students* will want to choose an author for a class study.

Activity

1. During the course of a week, read stories written by one of the suggested authors in the Literature Links section.

2. Discuss how one story varies from the other. Find out if there is something the same in each story. Notice characters, setting, plot, illustrations, etc.

3. Measure a piece of butcher paper to fit the door or wall. Draw columns (each to represent a different book). Print book titles at the bottom of the columns. Hang on door or wall.

4. At the end of the week give each child an index card or piece of paper. Older students will write about which book is their favorite and explain why. Younger students will draw a scene from their favorite book.

5. Each child will tape their writing or drawing in the appropriate column. You have now created an author story graph!

6. Read the graph to determine which story was liked the best and the least. Discuss why this might be so.

7. If you plan to do this activity more than once, laminate the butcher paper (with columns drawn), and write book titles on sentence strips or index cards. Use Fun Tac™ to replace title cards.

Extension Activities

- Using the pictures drawn for the graph, ask the students to arrange each column in story order, from beginning to end. Summarize the story through the use of pictures.

- Make author/story "domi-know" cards. On one side of the card write the name of a book, author/illustrator. On the other draw or reproduce a scene or character from the same or different book. Follow the rules for playing the regular domino game. You also can use authors on one side and names of books on the other side.

Literature Links

Here is a list of some of children's best-loved authors:

Harry Allard
Eric Carle
Don Freeman
Paul Galdone
Theodore S. Geisel
*   (Dr. Seuss)*
Russell Hoban
Arnold Lobel
Robert McCloskey
Tomie de Paola
Peggy Parish
Maurice Sendak
Judith Viorst
Bernard Waber
Charlotte Zolotow

60. Phonics Can Be Really "Phun"

Materials
- 4" x 6" (10.16 x 15.24 cm) index cards without lines
- markers

Circle Time Talk
Phonics is one of the basic language elements for constructing meaning. The story-books you read to your students at circle time will sometimes provide more coherent text (which will contain more clues to pronunciation and meaning) than the unnatural sound-ing text in beginning primers. But there *are* writers out there who write vivid, colorful stories for young readers and still use the controlled vocabulary of a beginning basal reader. During circle time, read and enjoy one of the Literature Links selections or any other favorite story told in simple language.

Activity
1. Prepare in advance for this activity by reading through your chosen story and choos-ing 15-20 easily illustrated words with initial consonants from the text. Do a simple drawing of the object and write the word below.

2. Read the story through a second time. After you read a sentence containing a word you have illustrated, hold up your card.

3. Reinforce the initial consonant letter-sound relationship by asking first, "What's this?" After your group responds ask, "Can you read the word below the picture?" After they have read the word, invite them to tell you what *sound* the word begins with, then what *letter* makes that sound.

4. Repeat this procedure until you have shared all your cards.

Extension Activity
- Use this simple procedure to teach short vowel sounds, then long vowel sounds.

Literature Links

The Very Hungry Caterpillar. *Eric Carle. New York: Putnam, 1981. Eric Carle's wonderful illus-trations bring this simple story to life. And there are lots of things for you to illustrate for your story cards.*

Cat Goes Fiddle-i-fee. *Paul Galdone. New York: Clarion Books, 1985. What a fun book! You can read it, sing it and dance it. It contains simple, predictable lan-guage and big, happy illustrations.*

The Cake That Mack Ate. *Rose Robart. New York: The Atlantic Monthly Press, 1986. Boy, that Mack is some kind of bad dog! The simple, predictable language earns this book an A for this activity.*

The Cat in the Hat. *Theodore S. Geisel. Boston: Houghton Mifflin, 1957. Any of Dr. Seuss's books would be great choices for this activity. He was the master of weaving sim-ple language into a rich and lively story.*

61. Animal Alliteration

Materials
- 1 piece of paper per student
- magazines
- crayons
- glue

Circle Time Talk

Read one or two books that are rich in alliteration to your students. Suggestions are given in the Literature Links. Talk about how much fun it is to say silly things like "Peter Piper picked a peck of pickled peppers" or "Andy Antelope ate his Aunt Annie's ant farm"! Tell your students that this technique for using language has a name, and that name is *alliteration*. Alliteration is *amazing* and *amusing*.

Activity

1. Read *Animalia* or any of the other Literature Links titles to the students. Have them pick letters out of a hat to determine what letter they will be working with. You may want to do the letters *Q, X, Z* and *V* as a class for demonstration purposes.

2. Have each student write his assigned letter on a piece of paper. (The teacher can write the letters on paper beforehand to make the finished product more uniform.) Then they make up a sentence using their assigned letter. Example: "An ape ate an apple in August." Have them illustrate their sentence by cutting pictures from magazines or drawing them on their own.

3. Punch out three holes on the sides of the papers. Then thread a piece of yarn or string to hold the book together. You may want to make your own cover or give that to a student as a special assignment.

4. Share the final product with the class or other classes. Keep it in a place of honor.

Extension Activities

- This can be greatly simplified and adapted for your prereaders. Allow them to pull a letter from the hat, but instead of asking them to write a whole sentence, ask them to think of one or two *words* that begin with the same letter. Your students can color a picture of one of their words, and you can write the words at the bottom of the page for them.

- Have students learn poems like "Peter Piper" to recite in class.

- Read other books by Graeme Base.

Literature Links
Peter Piper's Alphabet. *Marcia Brown. New York: Charles Scribner's Sons, 1959. This book is filled with quatrains of the same pattern like "Peter Piper." Students can dictate new alliterations as they become familiar with the ones in this book.*

Alligators All Around: An Alphabet Book. *Maurice Sendak. New York: Harper & Row Publishers, Inc., 1962. Alligators engage in alliteration nonsense.*

A My Name Is Alice. *Jane Bayer. Illustrations by Steven Kellogg. New York: Dial Books for Young Readers, 1984. A very funny and richly illustrated animal alliteration alphabet book.*

Animalia. *Graeme Base. New York: Abrams Publishing, 1986. This book uses animals to exemplify alliteration.*

62. On the Ball with Blends

Words for your blend ball:

sweet	green
stop	grass
street	grand
straw	glad
storm	glitter
stew	freckle
state	free
spring	fly
spot	flag
spill	flower
spell	drive
snip	drop
snack	dress
slip	cry
slide	cream
skate	cross
proud	crown
prize	cliff
prince	climb
princess	clothes
plume	clean
plate	brush
plastic	brown
play	bridge
gray	bread
grizzly	blue
group	black
ground	blow
grin	block

Literature Links

Strega Nona. *Tomie de Paola. Englewood Cliffs: Prentice Hall, 1975. Invite students to identify the initial blends in the main character's name and throughout the story.*

My Grandson Lew.

Charlotte Zolotow. New York: Harper & Row, 1974. Discuss the many words that contain initial and final blends in the story.

Here's a flexible idea that you will love!

Materials
- lists of blends: bl, br, cr, cl, dr, gl, gr, fl, fr, pr, st, sl, sp, pl, str, sw, squ, sn, sk
- large ball
- masking tape

Circle Time Talk
This is your time to introduce the concept of blends to your students (or whatever concept you decide to reinforce with this activity). Read *Strega Nona* or another classroom favorite to your group, once through for pure pleasure, then a second time pointing out the consonant blends. Ask children to repeat the blend sound after you. Explain that a blend is when two or three consonants get together but keep their own "personality" (phonetic sound). (As opposed to a digraph, when consonants get together and form a unique, new phonetic sound, i.e., *sh, th* and *ch*.)

Activity
1. Print different words containing blends on strips of masking tape and attach them randomly to a large ball.

2. Direct students to form a circle in the classroom. Throw the ball to someone and ask him to read the word that is on or near his thumb and then to find the blend. Example: If the word is *sled,* the student will give the *sl* blend.

3. The student holding the ball then throws it to another classmate and asks her to find a word. (Different hands and different fingers may be included in the game.)

Extension Activities
- The teacher may substitute other phonics skills such as vowels, digraphs, diphthongs, etc.

- Students can also be asked to spell the word, define the word or use it in a sentence.

- Spelling words or reading vocabulary words may be used in place of words with phonics skills.

- This clever activity is easily adapted for your prereading students. It can become a letter recognition activity by writing the letters of the alphabet on the masking tape rather than blend words.

63. ABC Ya! Creative Center

Materials

- letter blocks
- magnetic letters
- variety of stamps and pad
- Twister™ game
- variety of ABC books
  (various languages)
- alphabet bingo
- butcher paper
- pencils
- sand

- alphabet stamps
  (upper- and lowercase)
- letter cards
  (upper- and lowercase letters)
- wax paper
- ABC flash cards
- food coloring and icing
- chalk
- drawing paper
- variety of alphabet games

Circle Time Talk

Explain how to use the materials in this center. Review rules that apply when using various materials. Let students know that this center will help them recognize letters and form words.

Activities

Here are some starter ideas for you to use in this center.

1. Play tic-tac-toe using letters instead of *X*s and *O*s.
2. Play the Twister™ game with letters instead of colors.
3. Share an alphabet game with a friend.
4. Make an alphabet book with prepared papers that have alphabet letters on them. Allow the children to glue sand, macaroni, glitter, etc., over the shape of the letter. Fill in portfolio until all letters are done and then bind.
5. Make words using alphabet blocks or magnets.
6. Trace alphabet letters in sand or in colored icing on wax paper. (Yum!)
7. Use wax paper to trace letters from magazines, newspapers or handwriting books. Hold the wax paper up to see how well you can write your ABCs.
8. Put alphabet cards in order. Try it backwards! If you have two decks of ABC cards, play the memory game.
9. Use a piece of newspaper to find the letters *A* through *Z*. Start at the top of the page with *A* and continue down to *Z*, circling each letter as you find it. After circling all the letters, connect the circles and you will have a design.
10. Make a mini hopscotch board on butcher paper, replacing the numbers with letters. Hop on!

Extension Activities

- Let children write a newsletter to their parents discussing the letter or letters they are learning to read and write in school. Include in the newsletter words that begin with that particular letter. Children can practice this at home.

- Enjoy a snack that begins with your letter or letters of the week. On a cold day, try some alphabet soup!

Literature Links
Idalia's Project ABC—Projecto ABC: An Urban Alphabet Book in English and Spanish. *Idalia Rosario. New York: Holt, 1981. This book introduces the alphabet in English and Spanish!*

A, B, See! *Tana Hoban. New York: Greenwillow, 1982. Photographed objects, whose names begin with a particular letter of the alphabet, will delight your students.*

64. Phonics "Phun" Creative Center

Materials

- index cards
- sentence strips
- answer keys to appropriate activities
- picture dictionary
- drawing paper
- glue, scissors
- magazines, catalogs
- picture cards
- variety of phonics games
- writing paper and pencils
- vowel flash cards
- ball

Circle Time Talk

Phonics is the relationship of letter symbols and the sounds they make. This center will help you help your students recognize letters and give those letters sounds to put together to make words, words and more words. Keep this center updated with current (and previously taught material for reinforcement) phonics skills. Change activities as your skills change. Explain new activities when necessary.

Activities

1. Label items around the classroom (clock, art center, chair, desk, etc.). Make word cards for children to match the card with the labeled item.

2. Develop pages for children to identify initial consonant sounds (excellent for overhead). Example:

   1. Read words in both columns.
   2. Children will draw a line to match the words that have the same initial consonant sound.
   3. Check answer key.

dog	goat
green	win
went	yarn
yes	dig

3. Make a picture dictionary of consonant sounds. Use drawing paper that will be assembled later on. Fold paper in half or quarters, and in the right-hand corner paste a picture of a familiar object. Each picture must begin with a different sound. Cut out or write words starting with those sounds and glue in the correct place.

4. Use picture cards (cat, horn, telephone, crying baby, doorbell, tea kettle, jet, etc.) so that children can imitate the sound of each item. Older children can then write a sentence containing the word on the picture card.

5. Play a phonics game with a friend. These commercial games should be provided by you to reinforce a specific skill.

6. To reinforce the letter of the week, invite your students to list as many words as they can that begin or end with that letter. You may also use blends and digraphs as an alternative activity.

7. Work with a partner using vowel flash cards. Read the word; then write down words that rhyme and have the same vowel sound. Younger children can dictate a sentence to a classmate. Older children might like to write a silly or rhyming sentence and illustrate it.

Literature Links

There's an Alligator Under My Bed.

Mercer Mayer. New York: Dial Books for Young Readers, 1987. A little boy tries to lure an alligator from under his bed to the garage. Listen for final consonant sounds you know.

Oliver Button Is a Sissy.

Tomie de Paola. Orlando, Florida: Harcourt Brace Jovanovich, 1978. Oliver gets teased for not doing boy things. Enjoy this story while reviewing some vowel sounds.

The Costume Party.

*W.B. Park. Boston: Little Brown & Co., 1983. Help children find the sound of **y** as they listen to this cute story of a bear attending a party to which he was not invited.*

8. On chart paper, write mixed-up sentences for the children to rewrite. Example: the wash Mom clothes will — Mom will wash the clothes.

9. Write compound words and draw a picture of each word on a separate piece of paper (a finger and a nail; a foot and a ball) for students to match. Try this activity for contractions, too.

10. Use a bag, box or pattern (bear, apple, etc.) and write the sounds of the letter *Y*. Make word cards or smaller patterns to fit into or match the correct box or pattern. Example:

i	e	y
cry	baby	yarn
try	funny	yo-yo
fry	candy	youth
sky	tiny	yam

Extension Activities

- Go outside and play a game with a bouncing ball! Say this chant to reinforce the letter of the week or the entire alphabet:

A my name is Alice,	*(Bounce ball.)*
and my husband's name is Alan.	*(Bounce ball under leg.)*
I come from Alaska,	*(Bounce ball.)*
and I bring back Apples.	*(Bounce ball under leg.)*

- Use masking tape to write digraphs, vowels, synonyms, suffixes, etc. Tape letters or words on the edge of a spinning top. Spin the top. When it stops spinning, give a word rhyme, opposite, sentence, etc., for the letter or word that is closest to the ground. If you're reviewing short vowels, the student will then give you a word that begins, ends with or is in the middle of the word.

65. Hop to It!

Materials
- masking or electrical tape
- vowel picture cards (long and short vowel sounds)
- chips, pebbles or other suitable markers
- chalkboard, chalk
- stickers or small prizes

Circle Time Talk
Hop to it! This activity combines phonics with gross motor skills. Review the rules of the game of Hopscotch. Practice hopping on one foot and then two. Remember, children learn best by example—and they'll love it! This activity works best with a small group.

Activity
1. On the floor, construct a design of a hopscotch board with tape. Make as many squares on the board as the vowel/sound relationships being explored.

2. Inside each square, construct the letters the children will be asked to identify.

3. Children will sit in a line next to the board. Show each child a picture card. The child will say the vowel sound represented in the picture. If correct, the child will put a marker on the correct vowel on the board, then hop back and forth following the hopscotch rules previously presented. That child receives a point. (Keep score on the board.) If the child gives an incorrect answer, tell the child the correct answer and allow the child to hop on the board. The child with the most points wins. Reward all students with stickers and the overall winner with something extra.

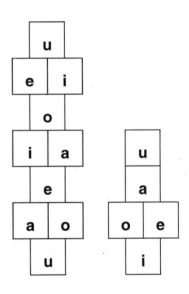

Extension Activities
- Use this game to help reinforce beginning, medial and ending sounds, letter identification and number recognition, too!

- Use the same hopscotch board or construct a new board. Remove letters (if appropriate) and begin with a blank hopscotch board. Focus on one set of vowel sounds (or letters for recognition). Show children picture cards with a certain vowel sound. If they answer correctly, they place an index card with that vowel in the first box. If they answer incorrectly, that box does not get a card. Continue game until all boxes have been gone through. Children then hop on the boxes with the cards (tape cards down) and repeat their vowel sounds.

Literature Links
Harold's ABC.
Crockett Johnson. New York: Harper & Row, 1963. Harold is at it again with his purple crayon. This time he helps us with our alphabet.

The Cat in the Hat.
*Theodore S. Geisel. New York: Random House, 1957. This well-known cat makes a rainy day an exciting day. Words like **cat** and **hat** help to review the short **a** sound.*

Go, Dog, Go! *P.D. Eastman. New York: Random House, 1961. High-spirited dogs help young readers to understand antonyms. Words like **go** and **dog** help children understand the long and short **o** sounds.*

66. Phonics Bingo

Materials
- blank bingo sheets
- pencils
- any suitable marker
- picture cards reviewing regular, double vowels (ai, ay, ee, ea, ie, oe, ou, oa, oo)
- chalkboard, chalk

Circle Time Talk
This activity is focused on reviewing regular double vowels but can be adapted to any phonics skill. Explain to the children that you will say some riddles aloud. The answer to each riddle will contain vowel sounds. Example: "It grows on your head." *(hair)* Show the picture that answers the riddle, and write the words on the chalkboard. Review all words once more underlining the double vowels. Remind students about the rule that states, "When two vowels go walking, the first one does the talking."

Activity
1. Review double vowel sounds with your students. Write the double vowels on the chalkboard.

2. Give each child a blank bingo sheet. Dictate the vowel sounds to your students, and allow them to write the double vowels on their blank sheets. Because there are twenty-four blank squares on the bingo cards, you will need to instruct your students to use each double vowel more than once. Example: "Write three *oo*'s on your bingo card." This way each child's card will be slightly different.

B	I	N	G	O
ou	ai	ay	ai	ie
oa	ea	ei	ee	ay
ou	oe	**FREE**	ay	ea
ou	oa	oe	ee	ee
oa	oe	ie	ea	ou

Example

3. Show picture cards of double vowel words, and the children will place a marker on their papers if that vowel combination appears on their cards.

4. The teacher will continue to show picture cards until someone calls out "Bingo!" Remind students to leave their markers in place until the pictures have been compared with the "winner's" paper.

5. A new game can then be started.

Extension Activities
- Play Phonics Bingo to help reinforce beginning, medial and ending sounds. This game may also help to review blends, diphthongs, digraphs, antonyms and synonyms. The possibilities are endless!

- Change the bingo game sheet into a basketball court or a golf course. Inside the shape of a basketball or golf ball, children will write the letter sounds you wish to review. As with bingo, everyone's paper should be different. The game will be played just like bingo, but instead of yelling "Bingo!" the children will shout "Goal!" or "Hole in one!" Variety is the spice of life!

Literature Links
The Three Billy Goats Gruff. Paul Galdone. New York: Clarion, 1973. Children will enjoy finding out how three billy goats trick a mean, ugly troll. The vowel sounds of oa and ee are nicely integrated.

Bringing the Rain to Kapiti Plain. Verna Aardema. New York: Dial Press Books for Young Readers, 1981. A clever Ki Pat brings needed rain to Kapiti Plain. The vowel sound of ai is repeated in this story.

The Queen of Eene. Jack Prelutsky. New York: Greenwillow, 1978. This humorous collection of poems describes strange characters, like a queen who likes to brush her teeth with onion juice. Have you ever seen such a thing?

67. Greeting the Seasons

Materials

- seasonal items (plastic or real)
  winter – hat, mitten, scarf
  spring – flower, egg, butterfly
  summer – ball, pail, shovel
  fall – twig, leaf, bark, acorn
- paper bag

Circle Time Talk

Read suggested material from the Literature Links to your class at appropriate times of the year. Discuss the things you see in your world during a particular time of the year. "Why wouldn't you see a snowman in the summer?" is an example of the type of question to ask your students. Seasonal movement activities could be a melting snowman, a caterpillar changing into a butterfly, a sand castle being made or a leaf falling from a tree.

Activity

1. Spread seasonal items or objects on a table. Have children feel and describe them as you identify each item.

2. Place items in a paper bag. Choose a volunteer to reach in the bag (without looking) and recite the sound that item begins with. Example: If a child reaches into the "winter bag" and feels a mitten, the child says "mmm." The class then tries to guess what item the volunteer is holding in the bag. The child then removes the item and shows it to the class.

3. Continue activity until all items are out of the bag.

Extension Activities

- Write an acrostic poem for an item that was in the bag.
  Example:

  My hand
  Is warm
  The other is lost
  Tried to find it
  Eventually got a
  New pair.

- Sing some silly songs! "Willoughby, Wallaby, Woo" on *Singable Songs* and "Shake My Sillies Out" on *More Singable Songs* by Raffi will help reinforce beginning letter sounds of *W, S, C, J* and *Y*. Add your own lyrics to reinforce any letter of the alphabet you wish.

Literature Links

Singable Songs and ***More Singable Songs.*** *Raffi. Troubadour Records, Ltd. Ontario, Canada, 1977. You'll clap and sing to the rhythm and beat that helps develop oral language.*

Here are some seasonal titles to choose from:

Curious George Flies a Kite. *Margret Rey. Boston: Houghton Mifflin Company, 1958.*

Cloudy with a Chance of Meatballs. *Judi Barrett. New York: Macmillan Book Company, 1978.*

Beany and Scamp. *Lisa Bassett. New York: Dodd, Mead & Company, 1987.*

Stopping by the Woods on a Snowy Evening. *Robert Frost. Illustrated by Susan Jeffers. New York: E.P. Dutton, 1978.*

Timothy Goes to School. *Rosemary Wells. New York: Dial Books for Young Readers.*

Jesse Bear, What Will You Wear? *Nancy White Carlstrom. New York: Macmillan Publishing Company, 1986.*

68. Letter of the Week

Materials

- magazines, newspapers
- old lunch boxes, containers (from oatmeal, ice tea, etc.) or shoe boxes
- clay
- shapes (circle, oval, square, rectangle)
- various patterns (flower, kite, sun, etc.)
- tagboard

- letter cookie cutters
- heavy string or yarn
- sandpaper
- chart paper
- scissors
- glue

Circle Time Talk

Reading begins with learning the ABCs. When introducing or reinforcing a particular letter and its sound relationship, concentrate on that skill for a week (for younger children) or a day (for older children), depending on your goals and the students' needs. Share the delight in learning using alphabet books that are not written in the same old vein (see Literature Links). Create a class alphabet book. Base it on humor, multicultural awareness or a theme (see Extension Activities).

Activity

- Have children bring in old lunch boxes or containers. Send the lunch boxes home with the students with a note for parents explaining the letter the children are learning. Encourage them to fill the lunch boxes with items from home that begin with that letter or letter sound. Then share lunch box contents with the class. (If a container is being used, punch holes in the sides and use string to make a handle.)

Extension Activities

- Go for a walk and look for things that begin with a certain letter. Write the findings on chart paper and display it in the classroom.

- Find different styles of a certain letter. If the letter is made up of mostly curved lines, paste it in a circle or oval. If the letter is made mostly of straight lines, paste it in a square or rectangle.

- Look through magazine story titles or ads, newspaper headlines and the comic section. Circle words that begin with a particular letter.

- Cut out pictures that begin with *B* and put in a box. Place *C* words in a cup and so on.

- Inside a particular shape, write words that begin with the same sound. For example, write *cat, cup, cow, cake, car, coat* inside a circle.

Literature Links

From Letter to Letter. *T. Sloat. New York: E.P. Dutton, 1989. Lower- and uppercase letters are surrounded by pictures beginning with that letter. The words for these pictures stretch across the bottom of each page. This book is a great resource for learning.*

All Aboard ABC. *D. Magee and R. Newman. New York: Cobblehill, 1990. Discover the world of trains with clear, focused photographs. Children might like to make their alphabet book using real pictures.*

Uncle Shelby's ABZ Book. *Shel Silverstein. New York: Simon & Schuster, 1961. A well-loved author shares advice to young readers in a humorous fashion.*

Jambo Means Hello: Swahili Alphabet Book. *M. Feelings. New York: Dial, 1974. Swahili words help to reveal the traditions of East African life. Use this book as an example of multicultural learning.*

69. Begins Like . . .

Materials

- chalkboard, chalk, erasers
- pictures with a variety of beginning sounds (magnet or Fun Tac™)
- spinner board (use the Twister™ spinner board and place letters on board)
- letter flash cards

Circle Time Talk

This activity invites the whole class to participate and have fun. Show the children flash cards with various letters for them to identify. When each card is shown, ask the students to identify, name and give the letter's sound. Search for something in the classroom that begins with that letter.

Activity

Literature Links

From Acorn to Zoo and Everything in Between in Alphabetical Order.
Satoshi Kitamura. New York: Farrar, 1992. This picture story alphabet book invites the reader to find objects in the illustrations which target a particular letter or sound.

Beni Montresor's ABC Picture Stories.

Beni Montresor. New York: Alfred A. Knopf, Inc., 1962. This book is filled with glorious colors and a type of puzzle format. Children will enjoy finding the arrows that point to words and identifying the objects.

Animals Around the World. *Robert Barry.*

New York: McGraw Hill Book Co., 1967. A variety of animals—all sizes, shapes and personalities—represent the letters.

1. Prepare the chalkboard. Write the letters on the board you wish to reinforce for sound identification.

2. Give each child a picture card or two. Allow the children to identify their picture cards aloud.

3. Spin the spinner. When the spinner lands on a certain letter, the child with the picture card that has the same beginning as the letter shown will bring the card to the board and place the card in the correct column.

4. Repeat step 3 until all the cards have been placed correctly on the board.

5. When the child brings up a card, ask her to repeat the sound of the beginning letter, say the word and use it in a complete sentence.

Extension Activities

- Choose one row of pictures to place in alphabetical order. Older students may form teams. Each team is assigned a letter. The first team to put the picture cards in alphabetical order wins. Then write the words next to each picture to double check.

- Use the same picture cards to reinforce ending or vowel sounds.

TLC10001 Copyright © Teaching & Learning Company, Carthage, IL 6232

70. MacDonald's Farm Vowels

Materials

- chart paper with song
- construction paper
- scissors, pencils, crayons
- large letters of the alphabet on poster board

Circle Time Talk

Have children sing the song "Old MacDonald Had a Farm." After enjoying singing it, tell them they are going to sing the same melody, but they will use different words about vowels.

Activity

1. Have the song "Mac Donald's Farm Vowels" printed on chart paper and display the vowel poster board letters from the alphabet.

   I can sing my vowels now – A, E, I, O, U!
   You can sing your vowels, too – A, E, I, O, U!
   With an **a** for cat
   Who jumped in a hat
   Here an **a**, there an **a**!
   Everywhere an **a**, **a**!
   We can sing our vowels now – A, E, I, O, U!

   For the other vowels use these lines:

With an **e** for hen	With an **o** for ox
Who lives in a pen	Who's wearing red socks
With an **i** for pig	With a **u** for pup
That's doing a jig	That jumped in a cup

2. Teach the students the song line by line by having them echo what you sing. Then group the students and give each a different vowel verse. On the last line, all join in.

Extension Activities

- Guide the students in making animals from the alphabet. Distribute construction paper and alphabet-shaped patterns from poster board. Have them choose a letter, trace it and turn it into an animal!

- Have students stand in a circle and mime the animal they created. Put on a musical tape such as "Carnival of the Animals" by Saint Saens.

Literature Links

Students will be motivated to imitate these authors' playful illustrations.

The Alphabet Symphony. *Bruce McMillan. New York: Greenwillow Books, 1977.*

Owl and Other Scrambles. *Lisl Weil. New York: E.P. Dutton, 1980.*

The Amazing Animal Alphabet Book. *Roger and Marika Chouinard. New York: Doubleday, 1988.*

71. "Tree"mendous Poetry

Materials

- pictures of trees from encyclopedias, calendars, magazines, nature books
- outside trees (if available)
- drawing paper, pencil, crayons, writing paper
- chart paper or a learning experience chart (large chart paper used to write poems, songs or brainstorming ideas to be shared with the class)

Circle Time Talk

It would be wonderful to have circle time under a tree for this activity. Begin your discussion by asking questions, such as: What kinds of things do you think about when you look at a tree? What do they look like? Sound like? Feel like? A tree can be a busy place. What kinds of things are happening up in a tree? Listen to your students' responses. Encourage each one to communicate something about trees. Praise them for their descriptive language. If you want to add movement now, get up and sway like trees in the wind.

Activity

1. Distribute pictures of trees from your various sources. If possible, take your students outside on a nature walk to discover the trees around the school. Students will observe the trees and brainstorm descriptive adjectives about them. Use a learning experience chart to record all responses.

2. Distribute drawing paper to the students and have them sketch their own tree, keeping in mind the characteristics described on the chart. Encourage them to draw the personality of the tree. For example, the tree might be a warm, friendly tree with birds and squirrels playing in it. Your students can draw a heart on the trunk of this tree. The tree could be a lonely tree with no living thing nearby (such as a weeping willow). In this case, the students might draw it crying and have its limbs holding a tissue.

3. Write on the board the following poem about a tree:

   > A tree is <u>nice</u>.
   > It is <u>tall</u>, <u>friendly</u> and <u>green</u>.
   > I love my tree!

Children can write their own poem by substituting new words for the underlined words in the sample poem. Tape the students' poetry papers to their tree drawings and display.

Extension Activity

- Throughout the year, have children draw a seasonal picture of a particular tree around the school. Use new descriptive words to characterize your "adopted tree." Maybe you can even give it a name!

Literature Links

The Giving Tree.
Shel Silverstein. New York: HarperCollins, 1974. This book shares a loving look at a special friendship between a boy and a "giving tree."

A Tree Is Nice.
Janice May Udry. New York: Harper & Row, 1957. This book tells the different uses of a tree and how it changes. The title of this book is similar to the first line of your students' poem. Discuss other ways that make a tree nice to know.

The Fall of Freddie the Leaf. *Leo Buscaglia. New York: Holt, Rinehart & Winston, 1982. This beautiful book relates the life cycle of a little leaf and its purpose in living. Picturesque photographs compliment the text.*

72. Adjective "Bag"-O-Rama!

Materials
- chalkboard, colored chalk
- little brown bags with small objects inside
- art paper
- pasta, pretzels, cotton balls, toothpicks, sand, cotton swabs, pretzel sticks

Circle Time Talk
Before class, draw on the chalkboard adjectives that resemble their meanings.

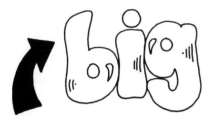

Discuss with students the definition of an adjective, and explain that it is a word that describes a noun. Show the adjectives on the chalkboard that are written creatively to look like their meanings. Ask volunteers to draw other examples.

Activity
1. Teach the following song to the tune of "On Top of Old Smokey."

   1. Some words precede nouns and can describe them.
      Like a *tall, yellow* flower or a *little, red* hen.

   2. They spice up our language and color our thoughts.
      When writing or reading what we have been taught.

   3. These words are called adjectives, so come let us sing.
      And talk about persons, places or things.

2. Organize students in cooperative learning groups. Give each group a small, brown bag with an object inside. Choose a writer for each group. Students then brainstorm adjectives describing the objects in their bags, and the writers record the responses. Choose a reader from each group to report the written adjectives. Now the class can guess the objects in each group's bag!

Extension Activities
- Provide materials such as craft sticks, cotton balls, pretzel sticks, pasta, etc. Distribute art paper to the students and have them choose an adjective to create as it looks. For example, cotton balls could be used to make the word *fluffy*.

- Display creations in a "Please Touch" area in the corridor or in the classroom.

Literature Links
The Rainbow Fish.
Marcus Pfister. New York: North-South Books, 1992. The Rainbow Fish is hesitant to share the gifts that make him special. Colorful adjectives help make this friendship story come alive.

Someday. *Charlotte Zolotow. New York: Harper & Row, 1965. A warm and delightful story with full-page color pictures and descriptions of impossible dreams becoming realities in a little girl's life.*

73. Kids and Couplets – What a Combo!

Materials
- writing paper
- pencils
- crayons

Circle Time Talk

Introduce the concept of a couplet to your students in this way: Read some of the Shel Silverstein couplets to the students and pick out a couplet that is particularly rhythmic. Pick two students from your group. Assign each student a line from the couplet. They will form the couplet and, holding hands, they can skip around the circle chanting their couplet. The other students can clap their hands to the beat. Repeat this in order to give all students a turn.

tune

June — (Moon) — spoon

soon

Activity

1. Read several examples of poems or stories using couplets.

2. Discuss the rhyming words in the story and write them in a "web." Give a brief sample web.

3. Lead students in recognizing two-line rhymes or couplets from the story. Write an example of one of your favorites on the board.

4. With your students, create your own couplets using words from the web. With prewriters, write the couplets on the board. Writers can write the couplets on writing paper.

Extension Activities

- Teach the students this song. Later on, have them substitute their own words in place of the nouns in the story.

Good night moon,   Good night light,   Good night wind-ows,   Trees good night

Good night room,   Good night bear,   Good night peo-ple,   Ev' ry where

- Have students illustrate their couplets using a watercolor/crayon resist technique and glue the students' handwritten couplets on the illustrated pages. Make a classroom booklet called *Classroom Couplet Caper*. Adapt this activity for your prewriters by writing the couplet on lined paper for them.

To bind your books, choose a paper size and determine the pages you will need. Cut two pieces of construction paper the same size as the book pages. Fold the pages of the book in half, keeping both sheets of construction paper on the outside. Staple or stitch the book pages and construction paper cover together in the middle. If sewing, leave at least 3" (7.62 cm) of thread free at both the top and bottom. Tie off at both ends and cut the thread. (Other methods for making books are on pages 32 and 57.)

Literature Links

Hop on Pop.
Theodore S. Geisel. New York: Random House, 1963. This Dr. Suess book shows simple rhyming couplets and is a good Circle Time Talk reinforcement book.

Good Night, Moon.

Margaret Wise Brown, New York: Harper & Row, 1947. This children's favorite is full of rhyming verses that are used at bedtime to bid "good night" to familiar objects.

Where the Sidewalk

Ends. *Shel Silverstein, New York: Harper & Row, 1974. Specific poems: "Side," "The Unicorn," "Enter This Deserted House," "One Inch Tall."*

74. Nouns, Nouns, Everywhere!

Materials

- pictures representing people, places and objects
- magazines, glue, drawing paper, pencil

Circle Time Talk

Introduce the concept of nouns to your students. Here's one way you might accomplish this: Prepare yourself by coming to circle time with a small toy, like a yo-yo, in your pocket. Sit down with your group and say, "Guess what I have in my pocket?' Allowing time for your students to say "What?," respond "A noun!" and bring the toy out of your pocket. Their response might be, "That's not a noun, it's a yo-yo!" This is your golden opportunity to explain that the object is a noun, too, because nouns are words that represent a person, place or thing. Teaching can be *so* fun!

Activity

1. Show children pictures of all kinds of nouns. Label the pictures. Use index cards to label nouns around the classroom. Have students place the cards by the correct objects.

2. Have children look through magazines to find pictures of nouns, cut, glue on paper and label them. When they are finished, they can come to the front of the room in groups. Then they can describe one picture from their paper by saying, "I spy something on my paper that . . . (is shiny, small and used to pick up food. Can you guess what it is? SPOON!)"

3. When this activity is completed, teach them this song to the tune of "Frere Jacques":

> Nouns are names of
> Persons and places
> And of things,
> And of things—
> Girls and kites and pizza,
> Boys and cats, and crayons,
> In our town! In our town!

Extension Activity

- Volunteers can come to the front of your classroom and hold up pictures of their nouns. The entire class will then sing an original version of the above song, substituting their nouns for the ones given.

Literature Links

ABC Book. *Theodore S. Geisel. New York: Random House, 1963. This alphabet book is a good resource for teaching nouns.*

Animals Around the World. *Robert Barry. New York: McGraw Hill Book Co., 1967. The letters in this book are represented by the animals themselves. Your students can identify the animals and reinforce letter recognition.*

Eye Openers. Farm Animals. Zoo Animals. Cars. Trucks. Diggers and Dump Trucks. Pets. Dinosaurs. Jungle Animals. *New York: Aladdin Books, 1991. Here's a great source for nouns with visual impact. Clear and brilliantly colored photographs jump off sparkling white pages with good descriptive text for young children.*

75. Nursery Rock

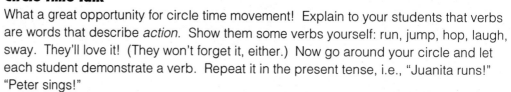

Materials

- various nursery rhymes
- writing/drawing paper

Circle Time Talk

What a great opportunity for circle time movement! Explain to your students that verbs are words that describe *action*. Show them some verbs yourself: run, jump, hop, laugh, sway. They'll love it! (They won't forget it, either.) Now go around your circle and let each student demonstrate a verb. Repeat it in the present tense, i.e., "Juanita runs!" "Peter sings!"

Activity

1. Review the definition of verbs and elicit examples from the students.

2. Show a video or filmstrip about verbs. Ask students to give the meaning of a verb according to the video/filmstrip.

3. Ask the students to think of their favorite nursery rhyme. Then they should take the rhythm and write their own rhyme using the definition of a verb. Example: To the nursery rhyme "Jack and Jill":

> Verbs are words
> That show action
> Like <u>run</u> and <u>jump</u> and <u>follow</u>.
> Verbs are words
> That show action
> Like <u>whistle</u>, <u>sing</u> and <u>holler</u>.

4. Share original rhymes with the class.

Extension Activities

- Use this activity to reinforce other parts of speech. (For example, show the section on adjectives and write the definition within the rhythm of a nursery rhyme.)

- Have students draw a picture to illustrate the rhyme.

- Have students substitute their own verbs for the "Jack and Jill" nursery rhyme given above.

Literature Links

The following books are nursery rhyme selections to familiarize the students with words, rhythm and rhyme:

Hop, Waddle, Swim. *Michael Berenstain. A Golden Book. Wisconsin: Western Publishing Co., Inc., 1992.*

Mother Goose Nursery Rhymes. *Arthur Rackham. New York: Watts, Inc., 1969.*

Mother Goose: A Collection of Nursery Rhymes. *Brian Wildsmith. New York: Franklin Watts, Inc., 1964.*

School House Rock! Grammar Rock Video with Cloris Leachman. *American Broadcasting Co., Inc., Western Publishing Co., Inc., Rochine, Wisconsin, 1987. This video explains the parts of speech in an entertaining way using music and cartoon characters.*

76. Blooming Ideas

Materials
- teacher-created patterns of flowers
- pictures of flowers
- fresh or artificial flowers placed around the room to create a more visual impact, if possible
- pencils
- scissors

Circle Time Talk
Read one of the stories suggested in the Literature Links or any other story that focuses on the symbol of a tiny seed pushing through the soil to the sunshine to grow into a flower, plant or tree. Discuss how your students are growing up, like the seed(s) in the story you just read. Do a movement activity in which your students crouch down low like tiny seeds and stretch up and up, breaking through the earth, until they are a beautiful flower basking in the sun's rays. Music would be a good addition to this activity. Play the "Morning Mood" from the *Peer Gynt Suite* by Edvard Grieg.

Activity

1. Show the students various pictures of flowers and discuss the characteristics of each one. Guide them to discover what flower best represents them—a joyful daisy, a pretty tulip, a tall sunflower, a lovely rose, a black-eyed Susan, a morning glory, a strong and hardy cosmos, etc.

2. Have students complete the phrase, "I am like a _____ because _____." They can then choose the appropriate flower pattern and write their response in it. Write the response on the flower for your prewriters.

3. Create a "flower garden" for your students by hanging these flowers on the bulletin board with a big sun and a watering can.

Extension Activities
- Make this a springtime activity. Students can create their own flowers from construction paper and crayons, and write their thoughts about flowers (or spring) in their original flowers. Display these on a bulletin board entitled "Blooming Ideas." Web your students' flowers around a large flower or sun shape that you have created. Label the center shape *flowers* or *springtime*. Prereaders and writers can enjoy this activity, too. You will need to write their verbalizations on their flowers for them.

- Customize this activity if you don't feel that flowers are appropriate. Use the same process with vehicles (cars, boats, planes, trains) or animals.

Literature Links
The Tiny Seed. *Eric Carle. New York: Thomas W. Crowell, 1970. Watch the natural progression of a tiny seed unfold a miracle of nature.*

The Carrot Seed. *Ruth Krauss. New York: Harper & Row, 1945. This book tells about the faith of a little boy who planted a carrot seed and the rewards he received.*

"I Am a Seed That Grows" in **The Mind Fitness Program for Esteem & Excellence** *by Caron B. Goode and Joy Lehni Watson, Zephyr Press, Tucson, Arizona, 1992. This story focuses on the symbol of the tiny seed pushing through the soil to the sunshine to grow into a flower, plant or tree.*

Acorn Alone. *Michael R. McClure. Virginia: A.R.E. Press, 1994. This is a good environmental tale about the continuity of nature and how trees protect all kinds of ecosystems.*

77. Short and Sweet . . . It's Complete!

Materials
- writing paper
- pencils
- crayons

Circle Time Talk
Read a simple big book to your circle. When you have completed one reading, go back and point out the uppercase letters at the beginning of some of the least complex sentences. Then point out the period at the end of each sentence. Explain to the students that a sentence needs a subject (a noun: a person, place or thing) and a verb (a word that describes action) to be complete. These two parts of speech will be a review if you have completed activities "Nouns, Nouns, Everywhere!" (page 79) and "Nursery Rock" (page 80) with your students.

Activity
1. Pass out writing paper and have the students write their first names on their papers (as many times as there are lines going down). After reviewing verbs or action words, tell them to write a verb next to their names. A different word must be used each time. You will need to write the verbs for your prewriters.

> Example: Kathy runs.
> Kathy jumps.
> Kathy eats.

2. Have the students draw a single picture to illustrate one of their sentences. Remind them that these sentences are "short and sweet and complete." Students can then share their sentences with the group and display their illustrated sentences.

Extension Activities
- Students can share their sentences by miming. Their classmates can guess the action that each student is doing in the sentence.

- Try recording some mini memories with your class. Create a classroom diary for a single school day starting with a cover titled "A Great Day!" Have each student think of an activity that the class has participated in that day. It might be something like "We read" or "We played." You might have now moved your students from present tense to past tense. Write each sentence on a separate piece of paper, and let your students illustrate them. Make a cover for your book and title it "A Great Day!" Bind it with yarn or brass fasteners.

Literature Links
Mine's the Best.
Crosby Bonsall. New York: Harper & Row, 1993. This book contains short and simple sentences. It is an excellent source for reinforcing this skill.

Good Dog, Carl.
Alexandra Day. New York: Green Tiger, 1985. This is a wordless picture book where students could write their own simple text.

78. Good Day, Bad Day

Materials
• 1 of the books in the Literature Links section or any other book that could be adapted to this activity about opposites

Circle Time Talk
Introduce the concept of antonyms to your students by reading the books listed in the Literature Links section (or other books dealing with opposites) to your group. Ask if anyone can think of a pair of antonyms, then discuss them. Ask pairs of students to demonstrate some antonyms, i.e., short/tall, high/low, long/short, happy/sad, laugh/cry, etc. This is a good opportunity to bring movement and expression into this activity.

Activity

1. Initiate a discussion about what makes the children have a bad day. Read the story about Alexander until the students are familiar with the repetitive phrase . . . "a terrible, horrible, no good, very bad day." Then as you come to the next phrase in the book, start off by saying "Alexander had a terrible . . ." Soon they will all chime in with "horrible, no good, very bad day."

2. Now discuss with the students what it means to have a good day. Create a phrase on the board substituting antonyms for the title of "Alexander and the . . ." Have them give examples of how Alexander's day would change. For example: "Alexander and the super, wonderful, awesome, very good day."

3. Have each child write a paragraph using her name and a series of events that would make the day either terrible or super. Example: Margo came to school and the teacher told her what a great homework assignment she completed. Margo was having a super, wonderful, awesome, very good day!

Extension Activity
• Adapt this activity for prewriters by having them draw a picture of <u>name</u>'s Super, Wonderful, Awesome, Very Good Day. Each child should share his picture with the class and verbalize the elements that made the day a good one. Take notes while the students speak and write their comments on an index card. Staple or tape the card to the bottom of each picture. Hang the pictures on a wall or bulletin board.

Literature Links
Alexander and the Terrible, Horrible, No Good, Very Bad Day. *Judith Viorst. New York: Macmillan, 1972. One day when everything goes wrong for him, Alexander is consoled by the thought that other people have bad days, too.*

Faster, Slower, Higher, Lower. *Michael Berenstain. Wisconsin: Western Publishing Co., Inc., 1991. This book is a colorful way to demonstrate antonyms.*

Go, Dog, Go! *P.D. Eastman. New York: Random House, 1961. In this book, fun-loving dogs illustrate antonyms.*

Today Was a Terrible Day. *Patricia Reilly Give. New York: Puffin, 1980. A clever story told in a witty way of a boy's day that goes from bad to worse. An ideal book to create an opposite version—from good to bad!*

79. Metaphor Madness

Materials

- construction paper
- glue
- scissors
- glitter
- markers

Circle Time Talk

Daily speaking activities are vital to your prewriters, and this activity will demonstrate the joy of finding rich and colorful ways to communicate thoughts. Metaphors are a good way of putting a *few* words together effectively before the ability to structure and sequence several thoughts emerges.

Activity

1. Prepare ten simple patterns, similar to the ones illustrated below, to use for this activity. Put lines for writing on each of the patterns.

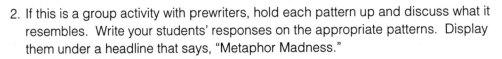

2. If this is a group activity with prewriters, hold each pattern up and discuss what it resembles. Write your students' responses on the appropriate patterns. Display them under a headline that says, "Metaphor Madness."

3. If this is an individual activity for writers, copy enough of the patterns to enable each student to choose one or two. Ask them to think about several things their pattern resembles. On the lines provided on their patterns, the students can write their favorite metaphors. Example: A star is the twinkle in the sky's eye. After they have written their metaphors, your students can decorate and color their patterns. These will make a great hallway display!

Extension Activities

- Have available the following ingredients and direct the students in making moon cookies.

½ cup (120 ml) wheat germ	3 cups (600 ml) dried milk
1½ cups (360 ml) peanut butter	¾ cup (180 ml) graham cracker crumbs
1½ cups (360 ml) honey	powdered sugar

Mix thoroughly and form into balls. Roll in sugar. Makes about 5 dozen moons. Eat after reciting "moon" metaphors!

- After the students have eaten and enjoyed their moon cookies, ask them to write or tell how the cookies tasted.

Literature Links

The Sun Is a Golden Earring. *Natalia M. Belting. New York: Holt, Rinehart and Winston, 1962. This book contains poetic metaphors from folktales about nature.*

"The Moon's the North Wind's Cooky" by Vachel Lindsay from **Silver Pennies.** *Edited by Blanche Thompson. New York: Macmillan, 1961. A well-known poem containing a metaphor of the moon as a cooky that is always delicious to read.*

80. Rebus Writing

Materials

- pictures of traffic signs, common symbols, animals, colors and numbers
- writing paper, pencils, crayons
- chalkboard and colored chalk

Circle Time Talk

Discuss with your students how people long, long ago drew symbols to communicate before alphabets were invented. Hold up pictures and have students associate them with words. For example, hold up pictures of animals, colors, numbers or common symbols. Students could create their own symbols and draw them on the chalkboard.

Activity

1. Choose a sample of rebus writing using one of the Literature Links ideas. Read this book and show students how pictures and words merge to make complete thoughts and sentences.

2. Encourage volunteers to assist you in reading the story. Prereaders can take part in this activity.

3. Distribute writing paper and encourage students to create their own rebus writing on a chosen topic.

Extension Activities

- Have students design a greeting card for someone who is sick, someone who is having a birthday or someone they need to thank. Encourage them to incorporate as much rebus writing as possible.

- Choose a favorite fairy tale, folktale or nursery rhyme. See if you and your students can create a rebus version of the story. Share with another class to see if they can "read" it.

Literature Links

Any one of the following rebus books would be a perfect introduction to reading for a young child. By reading the pictures, children delight in telling the story. Colorful art and entertaining text makes each of these books an exciting experience.

Read a Picture—Animals.
Burton Marks. New York: Smithmark, 1991.

Unriddling: All Sorts of Riddles to Puzzle Your Guessery.* *Alvin Schwartz. New York: Lippincott, 1983.*

81. Turkey Triplet

Materials
- writing paper
- tissue paper
- pencil, scissors
- construction paper
- turkey pattern

Enlarge and duplicate

Circle Time Talk

It's always fun to celebrate the holidays with young children. Begin this season-al activity with a good Thanksgiving story like one of those listed in the Literature Links. If you want to introduce some movement, gobble, strut and flap your wings. Then settle down and begin this fun activity.

Activity

1. Write this example of a triplet on the chalkboard:
   Turkey <u>green</u>, turkey <u>yellow</u>,
   Turkey says,
   "<u>You're a fine fellow!</u>"

2. Explain to the students that this three-line rhyme is called a "turkey note" which has been a Thanksgiving custom in Iowa since the 1890s.

3. Brainstorm words that rhyme with various colors, and write this list on the board. Example: blue/dew; pink/wink; brown/down.

4. Distribute turkey patterns, trace and cut on writing paper.

5. Have students write the "turkey note" on their papers, substituting their favorite colors for the underlined words above. Keep the second line the same, but end with an original third line.

6. Take this paper and glue it onto construction paper. Fringe the edges, wrap it up in colorful tissue and tie with a ribbon or yarn.

7. Use these for Thanksgiving favors at dinner or give to a friend.

Extension Activities

- Make patterns of a feather, a turkey head and feet. Distribute white plates. Have students color the inside of the plate brown. Make feathers, head and feet from patterns. Glue the ends of feathers onto the inside of the paper plate. Staple head and feet patterns to the plate also.

- Adapt this activity for younger children by writing this much of the triplet on the pattern for your students: Turkey _____, turkey _____,
  Turkey says, _____. Discuss options for filling in the blanks with your students, and write them on the board. If your students are able, have them copy their chosen words and phrases from the board. If this is beyond their skill level, write their choices for them.

Literature Links
These delightful Thanksgiving books are just right for sharing.

A Turkey for Thanksgiving. *Eve Bunting. New York: Clarion Books, 1991.*

Farmer Goff and His Turkey Sam. *Brian Schateel. New York: J.B. Lippincott, 1982.*

Turkey on the Loose. *Sylvie Wickstrom. New York: Dial Books, 1990.*

82. Label Fun

Materials
- empty food cans, cartons, etc.
- construction or drawing paper
- glue
- scissors

Circle Time Talk

Introduce this activity by reading one of the suggested titles in the Literature Links section or another title you have dealing with opposites. Reinforce this concept and enjoy a movement activity by playing a game of Silly Simon Says with opposites. (Silly Simon is *so* silly that when he tells you to do something, he *means* the opposite!) Example: Simon says reach up high. Simon says hold up your right hand. Simon says stand up.

Activity

1. Prepare in advance for this fun activity by saving food packages: cereal boxes, packages from granola bars, potato chips, processed cheese, whole wheat crackers.

2. Have a discussion with your students about their favorite foods. Why are these foods so good? Is it their taste? The way they look? Or could it be a popular food because of what your students have seen about it on TV?

3. Have your students work in groups to create their own labels on the packages you brought to the classroom, by thinking about the words on the old label and substituting opposite words. Example: Cheerios™ might become "Grumpios."

4. Children can then draw a picture to match the product's new label. Include size, weight, directions and nutritional information for the new label.

5. Share creations with the class.

Extension Activities

- ACTION! The children can make up a jingle for their new product. Have them act out a television commercial to endorse their new product. Example: (Sing to the tune of "Twinkle, Twinkle, Little Star.")

    "Grumpios" now comes in black,
    And you will not want them back.
    No fun taste, just boring food,
    They will put you in a mood.
    We're not kidding when we state,
    "Grumpios" are not that great!

- Discuss labels on packages, contents, size, weight, directions and nutritional information. Take a trip to the grocery store. Discuss how the labels attract people to purchase certain products.

Literature Links

These short, easy-to-read books will help introduce the concept of opposites to your students.

Opposites. John Burningham. New York: Crown Publishing, Inc., 1985.

Push Pull, Empty Full: A Book of Opposites. Tana Hoban. New York: Macmillan, 1972.

Faster, Slower, Higher, Lower. Michael Berenstain. Wisconsin: Western Publishing Co., Inc., 1991. This book is a colorful way to demonstrate antonyms.

Go, Dog, Go! P.D. Eastman. New York: Random House, 1961. In this book, fun-loving dogs illustrate antonyms.

Today Was a Terrible Day. Patricia Reilly Give. New York: Puffin, 1980. A clever story told in a witty way of a boy's day that goes from bad to worse. An ideal book to create an opposite version—from good to bad!

83. Making "Me" Books

Materials

- drawing, construction paper
- crayons, markers
- stapler, glue
- sample biographies and autobiographies

Circle Time Talk

This activity will enlighten students and delight parents. Talk to the students about being special and one-of-a-kind, using such examples as eye color, family and special skills. Sing this song to the tune of "Frere Jacques."

I am special.	*(Point to self using thumbs.)*
I am special.	
Look and see.	*(Hand over eyes.)*
Look and see.	
Someone very special.	*(Hands on hips, feet together,*
Someone very special.	*twist at waist.)*
Yes, it's me.	*(Bow or curtsy.)*
Yes, it's me.	

Explain that today they are going to begin to be bookmakers. The book is going to be about themselves and all the things that make them special. These types of books are called "autobiographies." Explain the difference between autobiographies and biographies by sharing sample books.

Activity

1. Make a list with the children, or use the following suggestions for the pages of the book.

   Cover *All About Me* by _____. *(Decorate.)*
   Page 1 This is what I look like in _____ grade. *(Draw portrait.)*
   I have _____ hair and _____ eyes.
   Page 2 My birthday is _____. *(Draw cake with*
   I am _____ years old.   *# of candles.)*
   Page 3 This is my family. *(Draw or glue on photo; label people and pets.)*
   Page 4 My address is _____. *(Draw or glue on photo.)*
   Page 5 My phone number is _____. *(Draw a phone.)*
   Page 6 My favorite color is _____. *(Draw or cut out pictures of color.)*
   Page 7 My favorite toy is _____. *(Draw toy.)*
   Page 8 My favorite food is _____. *(Draw or glue label.)*

Other "favorites" might include a place to visit, story, movie, holiday, shape, friend, sport or game. You can also include "Things That Make Me . . ." using such words as *happy, angry* and *sad.* The possibilities are endless!

2. Make accordion autobiography books.

Book Directions #1

1. For each book, choose as many pieces of poster board as there are pages of the story. On each page, use crayons to draw and write about the scene, or cut out and glue pictures from a magazine.

2. Create a cover which includes the title and student's name. Punch three holes in the sides of each page and the cover.

3. Use yarn, string or ribbon to lace sheets together.

Book Directions #2

Fold a 1' x 3' (.30 x .91 m) sheet of butcher paper in half and then into equal parts. A front and back cover can be made from construction paper.

3. Share finished books with another class. Display these books for Open House or in the autobiography section of the school or local library. Wow! What raves you'll receive!

Extension Activities

- Ask parents of students to write their child's favorite food recipe on an index card. Make a class cookbook. Send the cookbook home with a different child every other day.

- Using the tune of "Frere Jacques," encourage children to write a song about themselves. Example:

    I am Michael.
    I am Michael.
    I can swim.
    I can swim.
    I like cake and ice cream.
    I like cake and ice cream.
    I'm a boy.
    I'm a boy.

- Have a class pet show!

84. Write-On! Creative Center

Materials

- portfolios
- erasers, cloths
- Post-it™ Notes
- scissors
- crayons, markers
- index cards
- chalkboard
- typewriter
- envelopes
- computer, printer
- yarn
- stencils
- chalk
- dictionary
- stapler, glue, tape
- writing/drawing paper
- hole punch
- buttons
- old pads (memos, doctor's prescription, restaurant order pads)
- stamps (alphabet, animals)

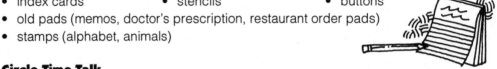

Circle Time Talk

Giving children the time and materials to write will enhance creativity and boost self-esteem, not to mention the progress you'll see in their reading! Show children all the materials in the writing center and explain their use. Remind children about rules concerning this area.

Activity

The following is a suggested list of activities for your students to do in the writing center.

1. Write text for a wordless picture book. Use Post-it™ Notes to write text on (easy on—easy off).
2. Write a prescription; take an order; fill out a check; write a grocery list, menu or recipe.
3. Write a letter to a sick friend, grandparent, principal, an author or a famous person.
4. Create license plates or library cards.
5. Draw a map from your home to school. Label all buildings and roads.
6. Write a mini book or poem about colors, holidays, nature, seasons, toys, etc.
7. Using stimulating pictures or seasonal word cards, children can create their own stories. Display child's story to class as Story of the Week.
8. Write step-by-step instructions on how to make a peanut butter and jelly sandwich. You could also provide the ingredients for making a sandwich. Let another student read and follow the directions given, exactly. Enjoy!
9. Make a class dictionary. Each time a student learns a new word, he or she can write it in the dictionary and draw an accompanying picture.
10. Write silly sentences using compound words. Example: Boardwalk—Did you ever see a board walk? Illustrate the sentence.

Extension Activities

- Cut a comic strip from the newspaper. White out the words. Photocopy the strip and make it into an overhead transparency. With the class, write new words to create your personalized comic strip. Older students may want to try one on their own.

- Distribute buttons to each student. Tell them to use their imaginations and pretend that they are that button on the outfit of a favorite character.

Literature Links

If You're Trying to Teach Kids to Write, You've Got to Have This Book! *Marjorie Frank. Nashville: Incentive Publications, 1979. This is a great book idea for teachers to help students through the writing process.*

Daily Writing

Activities. *Mary Hall. California: Frank Schaffer, 1988. This book is chock-full of creative ideas to stimulate your students' minds.*

85. Me, Too!

Materials
- drawing paper
- crayons, pencil

Circle Time Talk

This activity encourages students to share stories from past experiences. Discuss times when the children might have been late for a birthday party, had a new addition to the family or had a wonderful holiday, etc. Share a story of your own. (Tell the story about seeing a student at the store and he or she was shocked to realize you don't live at school!)

Activity

1. Choose stories from the Literature Links. Share and discuss the events in the story with your students. Make the events that happened to the character(s) more personal by asking, "Did this ever happen to anyone?"

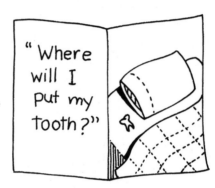

"Where will I put my tooth?"

2. Distribute drawing paper to students. Fold paper in half (like a book). Write a sentence or two on the board from the book for children to copy. Be sure to use quotation marks, capitals, correct punctuation, etc. Children will copy this direct quote on the left side of their papers.

3. On the right side of the paper children will write and draw a picture of a similar experience. Younger children may dictate their sentences for you to copy.

4. Allow students time to read and show their work to the class.

Extension Activities

- Make a time line of the story. Use a long strip of butcher paper for children to draw a mini mural. Begin with the title and author of the book. Choose students to draw events that happened first, next, then and last. Others can draw background and add designs.

- Show students a history time line of events. Then let them make their own lifetime line. Children can start by writing their names and date of birth; then draw a picture of themselves at 1, 2, 3, 4, 5, 6 and 7 years old. Fan paper back and forth to make a book.

Literature Links

The Amazing Voyage of Jackie Grace. *Matt Faulkner. New York: Scholastic, 1987. Jackie's imagination runs wild while taking a bath. Discover if you ever imagined the same things.*

A Chair for My Mother. *Vera B. Williams. New York: Greenwillow, 1982. This is a loving story that tells how a struggling family buys a chair for their hardworking mother.*

Little Rabbit's Loose Tooth. *Lucy Bate. New York: Crown, 1975. Children can relate trying to solve the problem of where to put a loose tooth when it comes out.*

When the New Baby Comes I'm Moving Out. *Martha Alexander. New York: Dial, 1981. A little boy faces jealousy when the new baby arrives. His mother assures him of special duties only "big brothers" can do.*

86. Overhead Projector Creative Center

Materials
- overhead projector
- transparencies
- tangrams
- permanent and nonpermanent markers

Circle Time Talk
Using the overhead projector is a different way to attract your students' attention to a skill or concept being taught. Explain how to properly use the machine and other materials. Discuss rules concerning this area.

Activities
Here are some activities to put in this center.

1. Use a blank transparency to draw different background scenes for a play production.
2. Create your own wordless picture or rebus story.
3. Photocopy activity pages that reinforce reading, language or spelling skills. Make them into transparencies for children to work on individually or in groups.
4. Practice writing a letter.
5. Create shadow puppets on the wall.
6. Write a class story on a chosen topic. Each child can write a sentence to help complete the story.
7. Display a poem for children to review parts of speech. For example: Circle the nouns.
8. Make a transparency of a brief story with missing punctuation and/or capitalization. Children can correct errors using colored markers.
9. Compare characters, stories or authors using a Venn diagram.
10. Create shapes of animals, things, etc., using tangrams.

Extension Activities
- Make silhouettes! Tape poster board or large paper on wall or chalkboard. Have each student stand in front of the projector facing sideways. Trace the outline of each child's head. Children can then cut out the tracing and write a cinquain about themselves inside their silhouettes. Prewriters can draw the things that tell about themselves.

- Enlarge patterns for story characters or write rules/notes concerning poetry, punctuation, etc., for future use to help save board space or for the convenience of not having to write them over again.

Literature Links
Shadows: Here, There and Everywhere. *Ron Goor and Nancy Goor. New York: Harper Junior Books, 1981. Photographed pictures of shadows help to tell us how they are formed and why they change.*

87. Can You Haiku?

Materials
- pictures of nature from old magazines and calendars
- art paper
- watercolor paints
- cut sponges and drinking straws

Circle Time Talk
Have fun clapping out the syllables of students' names to review the counting of syllables in a word. Use the names of pets, TV stars, sports figures as other possibilities.

Activity
1. Explain to the students that they will be listening to haiku poetry. Tell them that a haiku is a nonrhyming Japanese poem about nature. It has three lines with syllables of 5-7-5. Haiku poems are written about simple things, such as a bug, a butterfly, the moon or a frog. Have students listen to a selection of haiku poetry as you play Oriental music in the background.

2. On the chalkboard, write a haiku poem, and have students count the syllables.

   Example: 1 2   3   4 5
             yellow sunflower

   1   2   3   4 5 6   7
   burst forth from a little seed

   1 2   3   4   5
   rising to the sky

3. Sing it to this tune:

4. Write a class haiku and put it to music.

Extension Activities
- Students can create their own haiku on art paper and illustrate it using watercolors. Display their lovely creations.

- A haiku can turn into a tanka poem by adding two more lines of 7 syllables each. This version is ideal to write with a partner. One student can write the first part of three lines with 5-7-5 syllables, and a classmate can complete the thought with two lines of 7 syllables each.

- Distribute drinking straws and white art paper to students. Place a drop of India ink at the bottom of each paper and tell children to use straws to blow the ink up the sheet. Remind them NOT to inhale. As the ink spreads, it may resemble the bare branches of a tree in winter. What else can you see in the pattern? You may also give students cut sponges and have them apply different colors to the "trees" to create summer, spring or autumn trees. A haiku can then be written about their artistic creations.

Literature Links
These brief nonrhyming poems about the marvels of nature will stir every heart.

Haiku: Mood of the Earth. *Ann Atwood. New York: Charles Scribner's Sons, 1971.*

Cricket Songs: Japanese Haiku. *Translated by Harry Behn. New York: Harcourt, 1964.*

88. On the Track with Pronouns

Materials
- chart paper with song
- books from Literature Links

Circle Time Talk
Read the students a selection from Literature Links. Instead of reading the pronouns given, replace them with nouns. For example, "Ellen went to school one day. Ellen was so excited because it was her birthday. Ellen received a birthday button from the principal." Encourage students to tell why repetition of the noun *Ellen* is boring. *She* could have been used in its place.

Activity
On chart paper, chalkboard or overhead, print the following words that will be sung to the tune of "I've Been Working on the Railroad."

I've been studying my pronouns,
many times a day.
I've been studying my pronouns,
just to pass the time away.
Whenever the teacher asks me
to name them, I will say:
I, You, He, She, It, We and They!
Me and Him, Her, Us, Them!
They are substitutes for nouns!
They are substitutes!
They are substitutes!
They are substitutes for nouns!

Extension Activity
- Camouflage pronouns by writing them in other words on the chalkboard. For example: <u>i</u>gloo, <u>he</u>ard, <u>the</u>re, <u>m</u>i<u>t</u>t, <u>we</u>lco<u>me</u>, <u>she</u>lf, <u>me</u>at, f<u>us</u>s, <u>them</u>selves. Have students circle the pronouns as quickly as they find them, and have them think of others.

Literature Links
Can You Find Me?
Jennifer Deiney. New York: Scholastic, 1989. Students will enjoy finding pronouns in this science book about animal camouflage.

Teach Us, Amelia Bedelia. *Peggy Parish. New York: Greenwillow, 1977. An amusing book about the fun in having a substitute teacher who takes everything literally.*

An Evening at Alfie's. *Shirley Hughes. New York: Lothrop, 1985. Alfie and his baby-sitter experience an exciting night when the water pipe bursts.*

89. The Troubleshooters

Materials
- books from Literature Links (or any other storybook that places the main characters in a troublesome situation)
- chart paper
- writing paper
- pencils, crayons

Circle Time Talk
Ask your students to name some problems that families might experience at home or problems in the world that they've heard about on television or read about in the newspaper. Choose one of their responses and ask for possible solutions.

Activity
1. Explain to the students that they will be brainstorming solutions to problems that occur in the lives of some of their favorite book characters. Choose one of the books from Literature Links. After the story is read, help students identify the problem. Then encourage them to brainstorm possible solutions for the character. List their ideas on chart paper.

2. Distribute writing paper and pencils. Have students create a "Dear Abby" letter and sign it from one of the book characters experiencing a problem. Encourage them to design their own stationery that would be appropriate for the book character's use. For example, Little Red Riding Hood's stationery might be decorated with baskets. She might write:

> Dear Abby, How do you know who to trust? —Love, Red.

Extension Activities
- Display "Dear Abby" letters on a bulletin board or large wall area. Tape large, colored index cards under each letter. Encourage the students to write their own solutions to the problems experienced by the book characters.

- Encourage students to write a letter stating a problem they need to solve. Anonymous names could be signed to protect individual feelings. Watch the students come up with good written solutions. Students can put their daily problems in a "panic box" and the teacher can choose a few for Circle Time Talk.

Literature Links
The Fool of the World and the Flying Ship. *Arthur Ransome. Illustrated by Uri Shulevitz. New York: Farrar, 1968. In this Russian folktale, the Czar's daughter overcomes many problems with the aid of a wise old man and seven unusual companions.*

The Emperor's New Clothes. *Hans Christian Andersen. Illustrated by A. Rockwell. New York: Crowell, 1982. It takes the innocence and courage of a little boy to tell the emperor the truth.*

90. Journal Jottings

Materials

- notebook
- pencil

Circle Time Talk

Explain to students that a journal is a special notebook where you write your thoughts, feelings and opinions. Ask them how they would feel if no one came to their birthday party. What would they write in their journals about that? Have volunteers share their responses.

Activities

1. Have students keep a special notebook for "journal time." Designate a regular time each day for them to write some of their thoughts and feelings in this notebook. Journals should not be read or graded by the teacher. Have available a teacher's basket for those who wish to drop in their entries for sharing with the teacher.

2. Sometimes it is helpful to introduce topic starters for students to use. Some suggestions are If I were a butterfly, I would . . .; My favorite thing to do is . . .; Once I reached into my pocket and found . . .; If I could invent a toy, it would . . .; I would like my parents (or teacher) to know . . .; If I could make the world better, I would . . .; If I could have any pet, I would have . . .; Today I'm feeling . . .; The best thing about me is . . .; I like learning about . . . .

3. Ask students to give personal responses to the books they read. Prereaders can always draw or talk about their responses. For example, in the book *The Pied Piper of Hamelin*, how could the townspeople have gotten rid of the rats without the Pied Piper?

Extension Activities

- Have students pretend they are a book character writing a journal entry. What would they write?

- Students can dress up as book characters and read their journal entries. They could also hold appropriate objects that distinguish them from other characters. For example, Cinderella could hold a pumpkin or a slipper.

Literature Links

These read-aloud books are ideal for selecting a character for journal writing.

The Pied Piper of Hamelin. *Barbara Bartos-Hoppner. New York: Lippincott, 1987. The Pied Piper uses a lilting tune to rid the town of rats but is denied his just reward. The townspeople must face the consequences!*

Mufaro's Beautiful Daughter: An African Tale. *J. Steptoe. New York: Lothrop, Lee & Shepard, 1987. This African version of "Cinderella" gives a different twist to an age-old tale.*

91. Making Big Books

Materials

- large oaktag/tagboard 12" x 18" (30.48 x 45.72 cm) or 18" x 24" (45.72 x 60.96 cm)
- crayons
- watercolors, charcoal, pastel chalk, oil pastels (optional)
- binding rings or shower curtain hooks
- hole punch

Circle Time Talk

Good literature used in the classroom can serve to suggest ideas, provide models and give students a focus for their writing. Use the Literature Links suggestions to act as springboards for making class-produced personal big books about the children's own experiences. Example: The story *Brown Bear, Brown Bear, What Do You See?* by Bill Martin, Jr. can be made into *Kindergarten, Kindergarten, What Do We Know?*

Activity

1. Read a story from Literature Links or another of your choice. Discuss a related personal experience.

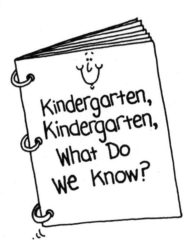

2. Pair the students up to illustrate and write one page. Revise student's work as necessary. Brainstorm ideas that pertain to the new story. Example: List things that kindergartners know. Next, list rhyming words related to things the children know (like shape, tape; letter, better). Help older students become aware of sentence patterns by counting the syllables of the original text; then compose stanzas together for an example. Allow students to work together.

3. Depending on the maturity of the class, you may want to introduce various types of illustration art techniques such as watercolors or pastel chalk. Allow the children to incorporate these techniques into their illustrations.

4. Bind the book together with rings or shower curtain hooks.

5. Share the book with students. Invite the librarian or principal.

Extension Activities

- Study works of a particular illustrator. Perhaps compare different illustrated versions of the same familiar folktale. Collect versions of "Cinderella," "Little Red Riding Hood" and "Hansel and Gretel." Ask children to compare the illustrations.

- Study bookmaking techniques such as papermaking, calligraphy, marbling, etc. Find examples of such techniques and share them with the class. Find and visit a book binder or printing press.

Literature Links

Good Night Owl. *Pat Hutchins. New York: Macmillan, 1972. This predictable book can be transformed into a big book for seasonal stories at Halloween or a science study of winter animals or other topics.*

The Berenstain Bears and the Messy Room. *Jan and Stan Berenstain. New York: Random House, 1986. Brother and sister bear have trouble keeping their room neat despite their parents constant reminders. Make a big book called "First Grade and the Neat Classroom" and teach those bears a lesson!*

92. A Special Class Quilt

Materials
- 6" x 6" (15.24 x 15.24 cm) pieces of paper (1 for each student)
- pencils
- crayons, markers
- butcher paper

- tape
- fabric crayons
- quilt
- solid sheets
- flannel sheet

Circle Time Talk
A quilt is made from individual pieces sewn together to form a whole. Much like a classroom of children. Each child is different, yet together they represent unity and wholeness. Show a quilt to the class and demonstrate how each piece makes the quilt complete. Read a story from the Literature Links section while children lay under or on top of the quilt.

Activity
1. Give each student a piece of 6" x 6" (15.24 x 15.24 cm) paper. Each paper should have a 2" x 2" (5.08 x 5.08 cm) border for the children to decorate.

2. Inside the square, children should write what makes them special and unique. Younger students can draw a self-portrait or dictate their sentence(s) to you.

3. Hang butcher paper in the hall or on your classroom wall. Tape quilt squares, side by side.

4. Draw *X*s on the edges of each quilt square to give the quilt a sewn effect.

5. Label quilt "Together We Are All Special."

Literature Links
Quilt Story. *Tony Johnston. New York: Putnam, 1985. A sad, little girl who has just moved turns to her patchwork quilt for comfort. Generations later, another little girl who has also moved finds warmth through the same quilt. A charming story for any child who has ever felt lonely.*

Sleepy Book.
Charlotte Zolotow. New York: Lothrop, 1958. The author discusses how animals sleep much differently than children. Text and illustrations are cleverly designed on black-as-night background.

Extension Activities
- Make a real quilt. Ask parents who can sew to volunteer. Cut solid-colored sheets (ask for donations) into squares. With fabric crayons, make pictures; then iron them onto the pieces of sheeting. Children then sew the squares together (with parent volunteer help). Use a flannel sheet as backing for the completed quilt. Make a book, using the quilt squares from the original activity. Children can take home the book and quilt to enjoy and share with their families.

- To vary the original activity, children can write rhymes, alliterative sentences, riddles, poems, etc., inside the quilt square. Vary the title as necessary. Examples: "Sew Many Rhymes," "Quite a Quality Quilt" or "Putting the Pieces Together."

93. Musical Punctuation

Materials

- simple sound instruments such as a triangle, drums, cymbals, wooden sticks, etc.
- teacher-made story with various ending punctuation included
- chart paper

Circle Time Talk

Let the children explore the musical instruments and practice playing them. Ask them if they ever played an instrument before. Which one?

Activities

1. Distribute the sound instruments to volunteers. Acquaint children with a teacher-prepared story written on chart paper. Put it on an easel and point to the sentences as you read them. Explain to the students that they will be providing the musical punctuation. For example:

   - A telling sentence ending with a period can be symbolized by a drum.

   - An asking sentence ending with a question mark can be symbolized by a triangle.

   - An exclamatory sentence ending with an exclamation mark can be symbolized (or "cymbalized!") by a cymbal.

   - Quotation marks could be symbolized by wooden sticks.

2. Invite students to choral read the story, inviting one volunteer to use the pointer.

Extension Activities

- Ask for parent volunteers to share their musical talents with the class.

- Sing a simple tune such as "Yankee Doodle" and have students use their instruments to the beat.

- Additional punctuation mark sounds can be added as the year goes on.

Literature Links
Good titles for use with various punctuation marks are

"Pardon?" Said the Giraffe. Colin West. New York: Lippincott, 1986.

What's Under My Bed? James Stevenson. New York: Puffin, 1984.

Wolf! Wolf! Elizabeth and Gerald Rose. New York: Faber, 1984.

94. Scavenger Hunt

Materials
- Scavenger Hunt directions (to be reproduced)
- pencil
- rewards

Circle Time Talk
Ask students if they have ever been on a treasure hunt or Easter egg hunt. What did they search for? Did they receive a reward? Encourage them to share their experiences.

Activity
1. Prepare a Language Scavenger Hunt for student partners to complete. Ideas for this activity are

    - Find a word that begins with the letter *S*. *(sand, school)*

    - Find something that rhymes with *sack*. *(rack)*

    - Find some items that contain a blend. *(grass, ground, tree)*

    - Find a compound word. *(playground, classmates)*

    - Find a word that contains a digraph. *(path)*

    - Find something that contains two syllables. *(cement, flower, playground)*

    - Find something that has three vowels in the word. *(playground, classmates, teacher)*

    - Find something with a rhyming partner. *(grass, class)*

2. Distribute written directions to the students and have them work in pairs. If it is a nice day, take them outside for the scavenger hunt. Offer simple rewards to the first partners that finish. Stickers, hard candy, classroom coupons for extra computer time, etc., make good rewards.

Extension Activity
- Give a scavenger hunt activity to be completed at home. For example: Find at home a snack that reminds you of a book character. (Fish crackers – *Swimmy* by Leo Lionni, Pantheon, 1963; jam from *Bread & Jam for Frances* by Russell Hoban, New York: Harper, 1964.)

Literature Links

If You Walk Down This Road. *Kate Duke. New York: Dutton, 1993. Travelers go down the road to Shady Lane with each bend revealing another lovely home.*

Rosie's Walk. *Pat Hutchins. New York: Macmillan, 1968. An unwitting hen outfoxes a fox while taking a walk around the town.*

95. Liters of Letters from Fantasy Island

Materials
- writing paper
- clear, plastic bottles (1 liter)
- note paper
- yarn
- treasure chest box
- drawing paper
- pencil, crayons

Circle Time Talk
Ask students if they ever thought what it would be like to live without any adults and be able to do anything they wanted. What might they do? What would they eat, and how would they get it? What would they wear? How would they spend their time? Where would they sleep?

Activity

1. Tell the children to imagine living on an island alone. Their only means of communication is to write notes in bottles and send them along via the ocean waters. Distribute note paper and plastic bottles to students. Have them correspond with their buddies on other islands, and then attach the rolled message to a piece of yarn and insert it into the bottle.

2. Send the class's messages off in a treasure chest and have a "buddy" class respond and send the messages back.

Extension Activity
- Have students find islands on a world map and learn that they are pieces of land completely surrounded by water. Then have them create and name their own islands. What items would they need in order to survive living there? Prioritize the list and share results.

Literature Links
The Island of Skog.
Steven Kellogg. Dial Books, 1973. A group of mice, fearing a cat, head for additional trouble on the island of Skog when they encounter a monster.

The Little Island.
Golden MacDonald. New York: Doubleday, 1946. A small island comes alive throughout the seasons in poetic text.

96. Open Your Eyes to the Future

Materials

- lots of cardboard boxes, paper towel tubes toilet paper tubes, fabric and yarn scraps, etc.
- construction paper
- writing paper
- scissors
- crayons, tempera paint
- lots of tape
- colored strips of paper taped over a plastic fishbowl (imitation crystal ball)
- shimmering paper to stuff into fishbowl to give a futuristic look
- glue

Circle Time Talk

Ask the students if they have ever seen the television show *Star Trek: The Next Generation.* How was life different in that show from ours today? What do the students think might change in our world in the future?

Activity

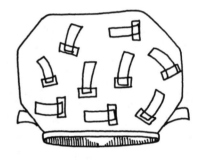

1. Before beginning this activity with your students, write ten to twelve topics on small strips of paper which you will tape to the crystal ball. Topics might include zoo of the future, human of the future, life in space, future foods, vacation on Mars, future fashions, airplane of the future, journey to the center of the seas.

2. Arrange the students in groups. Ask them to choose a category from the crystal ball and invent something from the future. Using the materials you have provided, students can construct their invention. Allow plenty of time over a period of a few days for this.

3. When the projects are complete, they can be displayed with a title and a few sentences about the invention. Prewriters can discuss their creations with their classmates.

Extension Activities

- Have students create a time line, extending it to the year 2010. What will they be doing? What will they look like? What will their friends be doing? Include illustrations and captions.

- Play a recording of "The Planets" by Gustav Holst, or try the "futuristic" sounds of works by John Cage or Phillip Glass.

Literature Links
Creating Your Future: Activities to Encourage Thinking Ahead.

Judith Bisignano and Mary Jane Cera. New York: Sheed and Ward, 1987. The edition for grades 1-3 is highly recommended for use with other future activities.

The Wonderful Flight to the Mushroom Planet.

Eleanor Cameron. Massachusetts: Little Brown, 1954. Two boys cruise the solar system in their self-built spaceship and have a great adventure.

TLC10001 Copyright © Teaching & Learning Company, Carthage, IL 62321

97. "Heart"y Messages

Materials
- construction paper
- scissors
- pencil
- crayons

Circle Time Talk

Have students share Happy Valentine's Day messages they have received. Explain to them that a *pun* is a play on words and is often used along with art to create a clever valentine. For example, a teacher might receive one that says "A 'heart'y hello from your valentine!"

Activity

1. Have your students use their imaginations to create a valentine for their favorite author or book character. The valentine message and design should have a clue to the character's identity. Example: "Wild Thing, I think I love you!" (a valentine message to Maurice Sendak).

2. Encourage students to read their valentine messages and have classmates guess who will be receiving this "heart"y message.

Extension Activities

- Have students brainstorm words with *heart* in them, and record answers on chart paper. Dictionaries may be used. For example, hearty, hearth, heartbeat.

- If you and your students are interested in sending "heart"y messages to a favorite author, you can address your letters to the author and mail them c/o the publisher, ATTN: children's books. The publisher will forward your letters to the author. Sometimes, authors reply.

Literature Links

Here are two good resources containing puns:

Caps for Sale.

Esphyr Slobodkina. New York: Harper Junior Books, 1947. A "cap"tivating story of a peddler who takes a "cap"nap and awakens to an unusual sight — monkeys wearing his caps!

A Toad for Tuesday.

Russell Erickson. New York: Lothrop, 1974. A "toad"ally awesome book about Warton who rescues a little mouse while on his way to visit his aunt.

The Valentine Bears.

Eve Bunting. New York: Clarion Books, 1983. This is a sweet, comforting story about sharing messages of love on Valentine's Day.

98. Tall Tales

Materials
- books of tall tales
- long butcher paper or computer paper
- pencils, crayons
- construction paper

Circle Time Talk
Explain to students that a tall tale is a brief story with exaggerated events. Have they ever heard of Paul Bunyan or Pecos Bill? Read them a selection from Literature Links. What were some of the unbelievable events that occurred in your chosen story? Cite the exaggerations.

Activity
1. Inform the students that they will be writing a tall tale filled with exaggerations about some made-up characters. Topics could be Gloria Giggles, Benjamin Bully, Billy Bookworm, Jenny Junk Food, Tanya TV or Timmy Tattletale.

2. Have students choose one of these characters or create one of their own. Distribute long sheets of computer or butcher paper for them to write on. Construction paper could be added to make a head for the top of the tale and feet for the bottom.

Extension Activities
- Tell students that tall tales and folktales were originally passed down by word of mouth from generation to generation. As each person told the story, additional facts were added. Play the Telephone Game. Whisper a message to one student and have him or her whisper it to the next student, who in turn whispers it to the next and so on. Have the last student tell the message that was received by the time it reached him or her. Had the original message changed?

- Using an opaque projector, enlarge a storybook character to the size of a child. Have the students create a tall tale about the character and improvise.

Literature Links
John Henry: An American Legend. *Ezra Jack Keats. New York: Pantheon, 1965.*

Flying with the Eagles • Racing the Great Bear. *Joseph Bruchoc. Bridgewater Books, 1993.*

Paul Bunyan. *Retold by Steven Kellogg. New York: Morrow, 1984.*

99. Knowing New Words

Materials

- index cards
- red and blue colored pencils
- small spinning top (i.e. dreidel)
- writing paper
- scissors

Circle Time Talk

Knowing new words expands a child's vocabulary and aids in creative writing. Read a suggested story, and ask the children to listen extra carefully for a word they have never heard before. At the end of the story, vote for a new word. Discuss its meaning. Challenge them to use that word as many times as they can during the day. Keep tally marks on the board and count up how many times the new word was used that day.

Activity

1. Write spelling or reading vocabulary words on index cards. Place cards facedown on the floor. Cards are in no particular order.

2. Spin the top on the cards. While waiting for the top to stop spinning, say "Round and round it goes, where it stops nobody knows."

3. When the top stops, one student reads the card which the top stopped on or closest to. All children will write that word on paper without looking on the card. That card is taken away. Continue until all cards are taken away.

4. Lay cards out on floor. Children will check their spelling. Rewrite any misspelled words. Then use red and blue pencils to rewrite words to show consonants and vowels. Use blue for consonants and red for vowels.

5. Younger children can vary the game. Spin the top on the cards. Pick up the card the top lands on. If they identify the word, they may keep the card; if not, put it back. The child with the most cards can be the New Word Winner for the day.

Extension Activities

- Add a fourth column to the paper from the Activity. Children can "box" letters to help them remember the shape of the word.

- Write words on index cards. Cut cards to separate beginning sounds from word family. All cuts should be different. Try to match cards together pronouncing each part of the word.

Literature Links

Geography from A to Z: A Picture Glossary. *Jack Knowlton. New York: HarperCollins, 1988. This alphabet book is focused around a content area–geography. Familiar and less familiar terms like* **forest** *and* **archipelago** *help illustrate and define the earth's physical features. What a way to learn new words!*

The Desert Is Theirs. *Byrd Baylor. New York: Scribner, 1976. Learn the words of the desert people like* **flora** *and* **fauna** *in this Indian culture-based book. Discover how their culture would live nowhere else.*

Digging Up Dinosaurs. *Aliki. New York: Crowell, 1981. The author discusses various types of dinosaurs seen in museums. She explains how scientists dig up, preserve and study fossilized dinosaur bones. "Dino"mite words are found in this book.*

100. What's in a Name?

Materials
- books containing derivations of names and meanings of names
- drawing paper or blank stationery paper
- crayons
- stamp pads
- ink
- colored yarn
- hangers
- magazines
- hole punch

Circle Time Talk
Ask the children if they know why their parents gave them their particular names. Were they named after a relative or a movie star? Does their name have special meaning? Encourage students to share their stories.

Activities
1. Research what each of your students' names mean. Distribute art paper to the class. Explain to students that you are going to tell them the meanings of their names. Have them write their names and illustrate their meanings.

2. A fun activity would be to call the students by their names' meanings for a day. For example, when taking attendance, ask if "a warrior" is present today. Imagine the look on Kelly's face!

3. Ask students to write a paragraph about the very first person with their names. For example, the first Robert might have been a very "famous" child because of his talents.

Extension Activities
- Have students put their fingerprints on their own stationery or greeting cards. By using a regular washable-ink stamp pad, they can press their thumbs or fingertips on the pad, then on the paper. Colored pencils or crayons can be used to add lines to change the fingerprint into an animal or figure. Placing two of these prints together can create figures with heads and bodies!

- Buy Bugle™ snacks and write the words *You Are Special!* on a slip of paper and stick it in the bugle. Give each student one as a treat! Have them "toot their own horns" about one thing that makes them special and unique, and share it with the class.

- Have students create a "Me" Mobile. Distribute hangers, construction paper and pieces of yarn. Students can cut out different shapes from construction paper and write various bits of information about themselves on them. For example: their names and meanings, their favorite foods, hobbies, members of their families, pets, etc. Holes can be punched at the top of the construction paper, yarn attached to the hanger and paper suspended from it. Students can illustrate their work, cut out pictures from magazines or bring in photographs.

Literature Links
Peter's Chair. *Ezra Jack Keats. New York: Harper & Row, 1967. Peter struggles to accept his new little sister until he finds the joy in the responsibility of being a big brother!*

"Rumpelstiltskin" in **The Complete Fairy Tales and Stories of Hans Christian Andersen.** *Erik Hougoard. New York: Doubleday and Co., Inc., 1974. The princess must repay Rumpelstiltskin for spinning her straw into gold. She must find out his name, or he will take her firstborn child.*

A My Name Is Alice. *Jane Bayer. New York: Dial Books for Young Readers, 1984. This fun book illustrated by Steven Kellogg is full of great names and colorful creatures.*